P9-CAO-939

Self-Employment:
From Dream to Reality!

An Interactive Workbook
for Starting Your Small Business

Second Edition

By Linda D. Gilkerson and Theresia M. Paauwe

DISCARD

jist Works

GREENWOOD PUBLIC LIBRARY
310 S. Meridian
Greenwood, IN 46143

Self-Employment: From Dream to Reality!, Second Edition
An Interactive Workbook for Starting Your Small Business

© 2003 by Linda D. Gilkerson and Theresia M. Paauwe

Published by JIST Works, an imprint of JIST Publishing, Inc.
8902 Otis Avenue
Indianapolis, IN 46216-1033

Phone: 1-800-648-JIST   Fax: 1-800-JIST-FAX
E-mail: info@jist.com   Web site: www.jist.com

Note to instructors. Support materials are available for *Self-Employment: From Dream to Reality!*, Second Edition. An instructor's guide published by JIST Works contains helpful guidance and many activities and assignments that can be used for adults. Call 1-800-648-JIST or visit www.jist.com for details. Coauthor Theresia Paauwe is available to "train the trainer" and sells a comprehensive trainer's manual. Visit her Web site at www.BusinessMattersTR.com for details.

About career materials published by JIST. Our materials encourage people to be self-directed and to take control of their destinies. We work hard to provide excellent content, solid advice, and techniques that get results. If you have questions about this book or other JIST products, call 1-800-648-JIST or visit www.jist.com. For information on 14,000 job titles, visit www.careeroink.com.

Quantity discounts are available for JIST products. Please call 1-800-648-JIST or visit www.jist.com for a free catalog and more information.

Visit www.jist.com. Find out about our products, get free book excerpts, order a catalog, and link to other career-related sites. You can also learn more about JIST authors and JIST training available to professionals.

Acquisitions Editor: Susan Pines
Development Editor: Stephanie Koutek
Cover Designer: Trudy Coler
Interior Designer: Aleata Howard
Page Layout Coordinator: Carolyn J. Newland
Proofreaders: Jeanne Clark, David Faust
Indexer: Larry Sweazy

Printed in the United States of America

07 06 05 04   9 8 7 6 5 4 3 2

All rights reserved. No part of this book may be reproduced in any form or by any means, or stored in a database or retrieval system, without prior permission of the publisher except in the case of brief quotations embodied in articles or reviews. Making copies of any part of this book for any purpose other than your own personal use is a violation of United States copyright laws.

We have been careful to provide accurate information throughout this book, but it is possible that errors and omissions have been introduced. Please consider this in making any career plans or other important decisions. Trust your own judgment above all else and in all things.

Trademarks: All brand names and product names used in this book are trade names, service marks, trademarks, or registered trademarks of their respective owners.

ISBN 1-56370-922-8

What Makes This Book Unique

Self-Employment: From Dream to Reality!, Second Edition, is unlike any other book about starting your own business. What makes it so unique?

- It is an interactive workbook full of helpful worksheets and exercises that get you involved in decision-making and show you examples of many aspects of running your business.

- It is based on the authors' proven self-employment training course and on their experiences as small business operators. You learn small-business basics through a tried-and-true approach taken by thousands of other would-be entrepreneurs.

- It is just right for first-time entrepreneurs. You learn what it takes to succeed in easy-to-understand language and without getting bogged down in hundreds of pages of detail.

You can turn your dream into reality. Let this workbook show you how.

Table of Contents

Introduction

In the early 1990s, Linda Gilkerson and I met while working for a microenterprise program helping aspiring and existing entrepreneurs realize and grow in their dream of being self-employed. Having both been self-employed, we shared a passion for fostering entrepreneurship. Together, we provided classroom training and technical assistance to hundreds of entrepreneurs, and before long, this book was born.

Today, microenterprise programs, schools, community-based organizations, and entrepreneurship programs throughout the United States use this workbook to help dreamers conceive and write business plans.

Self-Employment: From Dream to Reality!, Second Edition, is designed to guide you through the planning process by introducing key business concepts in practical, simple-to-understand ways. Worksheets and exercises are designed to encourage a hands-on approach to learning. By completing the exercises in each chapter, you collect all the information you need to put together a business plan one step at a time.

Whether self-employment is something you'd like to learn more about, a dream you've been pursuing, or how you make a living, you will find valuable information in this book. Good luck on your journey of turning your self-employment dream into a reality!

Theresia M. Paauwe, President and Owner
Business Matters Training Resources, Inc.

CHAPTER 1

The World of Business

Owning a business has always been part of the American dream, but today more people than ever are considering self-employment. Maybe you're thinking of starting a business because you've been "downsized." Perhaps you have the technology to work from home. Or maybe you just looked at the quality of your life and decided you need a change.

In this chapter, we look at the reasons people give for going into business for themselves. We explore the personality traits of successful business owners, review the main reasons that businesses fail, and look at how to avoid many of these pitfalls. And we show you why *planning* your business is not only time well spent but the only way to create a healthy and profitable venture.

In the space below, list all your answers to this question: Why do you want to own a business?

_____

_____

_____

_____

Of course, there are no right or wrong answers to this question. But your reasons are important because they will be the measure of your success. For instance, say one of the reasons you list is spending more time with your children. If, a year after starting your business, you find you are working more hours than ever before and actually seeing your children less, is your business a success? Or perhaps you want to own a business to make more money. If, after several years, you are still stretching to pay your bills, is your business a success?

One of the best things about self-employment is that you get to define what success means. And your definition is shaped by the reasons you want to go into business.

Before we go any further, we want to define two terms we use throughout this book.

- **Entrepreneur:** One who manages, organizes, and assumes the risk of a business or enterprise.
- **Microenterprise:** A very small business that operates from a home, storefront, or office and employs five or fewer employees (and often only one!).

Do You Have What It Takes?

Successful entrepreneurs come from all sorts of backgrounds and experiences. Age, gender, marital status, and education levels do not seem to be significant factors for success. But successful entrepreneurs share certain skills. As you look through the following list, determine the areas in which you excel and identify the areas in which you need work.

- What skills and experiences do you have that are key to the success of the business you want to own? Successful entrepreneurs have skills to sell.

  _____

  _____

  _____

- Are you responsible? Do you do what you say you will do when you say you will do it? Can people count on you? Entrepreneurs are responsible.

  _____

  _____

  _____

- Do you have good social skills? Do you say what you mean? Do you listen well? Entrepreneurs must be able to sell themselves.

  _____

  _____

  _____

- Are your financial and personal situations stable? Entrepreneurs need to be in good shape financially and emotionally to be able to concentrate on their new business without crisis in their personal lives.

  _____

  _____

  _____

- Are you optimistic? Entrepreneurs think positively.

  _____

  _____

  _____

- Do you have a strong motivation to achieve? Entrepreneurs are doers.

  _____

  _____

  _____

- Are you a hard worker? Do you work hard for others? Entrepreneurs often work more than 40 hours per week.

  _____

  _____

  _____

- Do you have problem-solving skills? Do you enjoy solving problems? Entrepreneurs are problem solvers.

  _____

  _____

  _____

- Are you independent? Entrepreneurs are leaders, not followers.

  _____

  _____

  _____

- Are you afraid of making decisions? Do you have a take-charge attitude? Entrepreneurs make all of the decisions for their businesses.

  _____

  _____

  _____

- Do you accept responsibility? Entrepreneurs accept responsibility for their own businesses.

  _____

  _____

  _____

Following is a list of personality traits that are common to successful entrepreneurs. How many of them do you possess?

- Motivation to achieve
- Capacity for continued hard work
- Nonconformity
- Strong leadership ability
- Street smarts
- Responsibility
- Optimistic outlook

Some personality traits are not conducive to successful entrepreneurship, including these:

- Compulsive in gambling
- High risk taking
- Impulsive or inclined to "shoot from the hip"

Finally, some factors are less important—they seem to make no difference to one's capacity for success:

- Age
- Gender
- Marital status
- Education level

Business Failure

We've all heard the bad news. Here are some common statistics that scare many people away from self-employment:

- One in three new businesses fail within six months.
- Three of four start-ups shut down within five years.
- Nine out of ten companies operating today will eventually fail.

Scary statistics indeed. But before you become discouraged, consider the fact that these statistics do not tell the whole story. Many of the "failures" are more accurately called "career changes," as no money was lost and the closure of the company was voluntary. In fact, many owners of the closed businesses considered their businesses successful but decided to cease operation for many reasons: the hours were too long, the market changed, or the owners could make more money by working for someone else.

So, although some businesses do fail, the chances for success are better than you might think.

Why Do Businesses Fail?

Why do you think businesses fail? _____

_____

_____

© *JIST Works*

Compare your answers to some of these reasons for business failure. Knowing some of the pitfalls *before* you start your business can help you avoid them. We address most of these problems in this workbook.

- **Owner's personality not suited to running a business.** Business owners who are reluctant to make decisions or who lack self-discipline have a greater chance of failing. Businesses run on relationships. Customers need to trust the owner so they will be comfortable doing business with him or her. A business owner who has difficulty getting along with people will be at a disadvantage.

- **Poor choice of business opportunity.** Some fields in the marketplace are saturated. For example, it seems you can't drive a city block without seeing a pizza place, an instant print shop, or a video store. Having lots of competition means that you must have something terrific to offer customers that your competitors don't. These are risky business ventures, simply because there are so many of them.

- **Inadequate start-up capital.** Many businesses begin without enough money in reserve. Chances are, finding customers and generating enough income to support the business will take longer than you expect. On the other hand, if you make good decisions when spending your start-up capital, you may actually need less money than you originally estimate.

  In the beginning, invest your cash in people and things that will result in sales—not in "flash." Forget the fancy office and the latest gadgets *unless they are absolutely necessary to make sales.* Sometimes leasing or renting equipment can save you money during the start-up phase. Ask yourself this question before you buy anything: How will this expenditure result in sales?

- **Poor selection of location.** If you are locating your business outside your home, choose your spot based on where your customers live, shop, or visit. Do not base this decision on proximity to your home. Don't take a space simply because it happens to be available on the first day you're looking. Try to leave your emotions out of the decision. This is especially important for retail businesses. When you're looking at a potential spot, ask yourself this question: Will this location result in sales?

- **Lack of knowledge about attracting customers.** You must have a plan to get customers to try your product or service. You can't simply offer lower prices than your competitors and be successful. Remember, consumers are creatures of habit. They must have a reason to change their spending habits.

- **Failure to seek professional advice.** It is critical that you seek the advice of an accountant and, depending on your business, an attorney. Save yourself grief by finding and hiring an accountant in the beginning. Your business may also require other professionals. You probably have expertise in the business you have chosen, but you are probably not an authority on every aspect of your business.

- **Poor choice of legal form.** You need to understand the different legal forms of business so you can make an informed decision about which is best for you. We discuss sole proprietorships, partnerships, and different types of corporations in Chapter 8. There are many factors to consider, and taxes are an important one. So this may be a decision you want to discuss with your accountant and attorney.

- **Insufficient experience in product or service.** Some people dive into a business without understanding how that particular industry works. As a result, they may set up a pricing structure that will not allow them to make a profit. Or they might produce an inferior product or service. Successful business owners either have experience in the industry or take the time to research it thoroughly *before* taking the plunge.

- **Insufficient planning and investigation.** Many people spend more time planning their vacations than they do planning their careers. Surprises will always happen, but if you take the time to plan, fewer issues are left to chance. Planning will accomplish one of two things: (1) You will decide that your business idea won't work or that you are not ready; or (2) you will be convinced that you have a good idea that can work, and you will be comfortable with the risk of self-employment.

> *Remember, a business owner who fails to plan plans to fail!*

What is your biggest challenge for business ownership? How will you overcome it?

_____

_____

_____

_____

Planning Your Business Is Critical

Many people float aimlessly through life, taking its ups and downs as they come, just getting by and living from day to day. If they become successful, or even comfortable, it's more by accident than by plan. This approach rarely works for a business.

Proper planning allows you to try out your business on paper with no financial risk. Your plan is your road map: It tells you where you should be at any given time, when you are succeeding, when you need to make adjustments, even when it's time to get out.

It's impossible to know everything you need to before going into business. The sheer amount of information is staggering. But you should figure out what you need to know before starting the business and then plan to continue learning.

> *Learn to plan and plan to learn!*

Your Best Bet Is a Business Plan

If you have spent any time researching self-employment, you probably have encountered the concept of a *business plan*. And if you are like most people, the more you read about business plans, the more confused you became. There are several different outlines to choose from, all with different sections. Some outlines use questions, some use big business words. And the main thing many people draw from these "helps" is that a business plan is very complicated. But it doesn't have to be. A business plan can be a simple, effective tool for planning, financing, and growing your business.

Before we discuss what a business plan should look like, take a look at why a business plan is critical to your success:

- **A business plan can give you the confidence to start your business, or it can help you realize that your business idea is not a good one.** Before you make the final decision, you need to think through the answers to many questions about your product or service, your customers, your pricing, your marketing, and your potential cash flow. Your business plan gives you a process for answering those questions in an organized and logical way.

- **After you start your business, you can refer back to your business plan to keep you focused on the next task.** A business plan is never finished. It changes as circumstances in your business change. You can use it as a guide to build and manage a successful business.

- **A business plan is a small business's best tool for raising money.** Most financial institutions will insist on a business plan to evaluate your idea. Your business plan gives the loan officer information about you and your idea and allows him or her to evaluate your business's creditworthiness.

- **A business plan can be a marketing tool.** As you write your business plan, you will have a clearer picture of your business. This will help you explain what services or products your business will provide, who your customers will be, and what your goals are for the business. Have your employees read your business plan so they understand what you want to accomplish.

The Contents of a Business Plan

You will find an outline of a business plan on the following pages. As you read it, don't get hung up on the information you don't have. This workbook leads you through the steps of gathering information for your own business plan, and we include a sample business plan in the Appendix.

Business Plan Outline

1. Introduction

Title page

Name of business and your name.

Your address and telephone number.

Write the words "Business Plan" on the title page.

Table of contents

Pages should be numbered.

General description of the business

Describe the business you want to start.

What services or products will you offer?

Where will you locate?

Explain why you choose this business.

What are the skills and experiences you bring to the business?

(continued)

(continued)

What are your goals for the business?

What is your action plan to achieve these goals?

2. Marketing

Product or service description

What is your product/service?

What is the demand for your product/service?

Market description

Who is your customer?

How do you know?

Describe any market research by industry experts or any research you have done.

Is your business idea a fad or a trend?

How will your market grow or change over the next few years?

Competition

List your competitors and identify their strengths and weaknesses.

Compare prices, product quality, etc.

What advantages will your business have over the competition?

Selling strategy

How will you sell your product or service?

What is your pricing strategy?

What advertising will you do?

What promotions will you do?

How will your product or service be delivered?

3. Organization

Quality control

How will you ensure the quality of your products or services?

Legal structure

In what legal form will you do business?

Why is this form best for you?

If more than one person is in the business, include agreements.

Insurance

What insurance will your business carry?

Management

How will your business be managed on a day-to-day basis?

Who will be responsible for monthly financial reports?

How will management change in the future?

How will your business records be maintained?

© JIST Works

Advisors

Who is your accountant?

Who is your attorney?

Who are the people you can turn to for good advice?

Other issues

Discuss any other issues pertinent to your business.

4. Financial plan

What equipment or supplies will you need?

What are your resources?

What financing will you need?

Cash-flow projections

Monthly: Use "best guess," "high side," and "low side" numbers.

Operating budget

Provide a monthly budget for the first year.

Provide "what-if" statements.

If you are using your business plan to request a loan, you should also include the following:

Supporting material

Brochures, business cards, summary of market research, references from people who know you or the business

Purpose and amount of the loan

An exact dollar amount you want to borrow for the business and a description of how you will use the money.

Explanation of your personal credit

If you have had any credit problems, acknowledge them and explain how you have resolved the problem.

Summing Up

Ready to get started? After reading though the business plan outline, you may think that it asks for more information than you have. This workbook will help you gather the necessary information and make decisions based on that information. Learning is like building with blocks. What you learn at first determines which questions you need to answer next. In the next chapter, you consider what business would be best for you, and we explain how you can share your business dream with others so they can catch your excitement.

CHAPTER 2

Defining Your Dream

Some people are very clear about the type of business they want to start. But it's perfectly acceptable to first decide that you want to start a business and then read, listen, and search for the business that would work for you. You should begin the process by thinking about who you are, what you enjoy doing, and how you really want to spend your time.

After you decide what kind of business you want to start, take time to daydream and develop a clear mental image of your business. Imagine yourself doing the business. This is the first step in communicating your idea to others. Write a brief description of your business and practice saying it. Select a name for your business; giving it a name will make it feel like a reality.

In this chapter, you identify the business you want to start and your support people for this new adventure. It is important to know who those people are *before* you need them.

A Good Business for You

To get started, read through, think about, and then answer the following questions:

- What are your gifts and talents? A gift is anything you do very well or something that comes easily to you.

  _____

  _____

  _____

- What are your passions? Does your life have a mission? Is there something you feel so strongly about that you want to spend your time convincing others of its worth?

  _____

  _____

  _____

- What have you read or heard that interests you? Spend some time reading and learning about what businesses others are starting. Be open to opportunities.

  _____

  _____

  _____

- What are your personal goals? Be sure to consider your lifestyle. It's important to select a business that satisfies you and involves work you love and do well.

_____

_____

_____

_____

_____

_____

_____

Where to Find Business Opportunities

- The public library
- The Internet
- Entrepreneurial magazines
- Newspapers
- Friends or acquaintances
- The Yellow Pages

Business Possibilities

List the business possibilities you are considering. List the advantages and disadvantages of each business. Consider start-up costs, hours, the type of work, and any other factors you can think of.

Business Possibilities	Advantages	Disadvantages

Narrow Your Choices

Talk to people in the selected business.

Read about those businesses. Try to find statistics about the businesses.

Ask your accountant or your banker.

Share your ideas with family and friends and be ready to listen to their reactions.

Make your final decision.

© JIST Works

25 Business Ideas to Consider

Antique dealer	Home inspection service
Auto detailing	Import/Export business guide
Child care provider	Information broker
Consulting	Landscaper
Craft business	Mail order business
Desktop publishing	Medical claims processing
Event-planning service	Professional organizer
Financial aid service	Secretarial/Word processing
Gift basket service	Sewing business
Handyman service	Vending machine business
Herb farming	Web design
Home computer operator	Wedding planning service
Home health care	

Every successful business starts as a daydream in the owner's mind, but most people get so caught up in daily living that they don't take time to be quiet and dream. The time you spend imagining yourself making your product or service and actually running your business is time well spent. Some people have such strong, vivid images of their businesses that they are practically compelled to start them. So get comfortable, close your eyes, and "see" your business. Take time to dream every day until your thoughts begin to seem possible and real. Use the following questions to get started, and when you have the answers, write them in.

- What is my business dream?

  _____

  _____

  _____

- Where is my place of business and what are my equipment needs?

  _____

  _____

  _____

- Who are my customers?

  _____

  _____

  _____

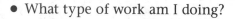

- What type of work am I doing?

_____

_____

_____

In later chapters, we discuss how to determine if your business idea will work. But, at this beginning stage, the best thing you can do is talk about your idea. Be prepared to listen carefully to people's reactions to your idea. Try not to take comments personally; instead, use the feedback to determine if your business idea should be discarded or if you should continue your investigation. And don't be discouraged if you discard several business possibilities before finding one that seems possible. Be prepared to take your time and think through each idea. To investigate a business, you must learn and listen; fortunately, both are inexpensive activities.

Describing Your Business

Spend time thinking through how you will explain your business idea to others. If you want someone to listen to your idea and react to it, you must be very clear in what you say. Practice your description often so you can describe your business dream clearly in just one sentence when you have an opportunity.

Communication Exercise

Read through the dialogue below. Imagine the patient friend's reaction to the business starter's rambling answer to the question "What is your new business?"

Business Starter: "I'm going to start a new business!"

Patient Friend: "Oh, really? What is your new business?"

Business Starter: "Well, **you know how,** have you ever, you know, thought about, um, starting to do something different in your life? You know, like when your job is a drag and your boss is a jerk and you aren't making any money, so you decide to start your own business—but, you know, think about how **difficult it would be if you decided that you wanted to go into business for yourself but you had no idea,** absolutely no idea. I mean, how would you? You know? How would you know, even, **where to begin?** Huh? Well, you wouldn't, because how many times before have you ever gone into business for yourself? Really! Think about it—it would be a totally foreign experience. Okay! So **even if you went to the library and read books about it, most of that material is written,** and I mean, I really know this is true, it's written **in business language, which most people don't understand.** So, my idea would be, I mean, if people thought it would work, I mean. I don't know, so, I'd have to ask a lot of people if they thought it would work, but if a lot of people thought it might work, I could do this. Well, I think I could do this, but anyway, **my business** idea **would**

© JIST Works

be to **provide training to people who have no idea how to start a business of their own.** After all, I've had my own business before, so I have some experience in this, and I have a friend who has had a couple of businesses, and she could help me. **And my training would be in plain English, using words everyone can understand,** because, after all, I mean, I know I'm a good communicator. I mean, don't you feel bad for people who really want to quit their jobs and would if they could, but they just don't know how to...they just don't know where to begin to, **and,** well anyway, **I would base the training around writing a business plan,** and we could talk about, oh!—and this would be really cool!—experiences other people have had starting their own businesses. And I would provide, you know, resource materials about how to name your business, and I could teach people about marketing and financial stuff, and, you know, all kinds of stuff that people would need to know, but don't know, you know, about starting their own business. You know? What d'ya think?"

Impatient Friend: "Have you met that new guy in accounting?"

Now, go through the dialogue again, this time reading only the bold sections of the business starter's answer. What is the friend's reaction now? It's important to practice describing your business as concisely and precisely as possible.

Here is a good practice exercise. Suppose you are being interviewed by a TV reporter. You have 15 seconds to respond to this question: "What business are you in?"

_____

_____

_____

_____

_____

Make a list of people with whom you want to share your business idea. Jot down their reactions.

_____

_____

_____

_____

_____

What's in a Name?

Everyone knows how important a name can be, whether you're talking about a baby or a new business. We all know businesses with great names (and businesses with so-so names). Be prepared to spend time finding the right name for your business. As you gather information about your business, keep tossing names around in your head. Be sure to write them down. A word you jot down today may sound great with another word you think of next week. Take time to select the best name for your business, because whatever you choose, you'll have to live with it. Make sure the name you select meets most of these criteria:

- It quickly identifies what you do
- It stands out from the competition
- It's easy to remember
- It's easy to spell and pronounce
- It's neither too short nor too long

First, **brainstorm** a long list of words that describe what you want your business to reflect. Think of adjectives, feelings, features, and images you have about the business. You can use a name that tells what the business does, communicates the primary benefit of your product or service, or describes the main activity of your business. Or you can simply make up a name.

Next, **piece the words together.** How do they sound together? Do they convey the image you want for your business? **Remember your customers.** Will they remember the name? **Share the best names with friends.** Listen to their reactions. Don't panic if you don't have the perfect name as you begin planning your business. As you gather information and your dream becomes more real to you, you'll find the right name.

Identify Your Support Team

The decision to start a new business is yours to make, but it's important to identify people who will be supportive *before* you begin your business. Although financial support is obviously helpful, you should also think about who in your life will give you emotional support, objective critiques, realistic views, and new ideas. You need people around you who believe in your dream and your ability to realize it. Having people offer enthusiastic support, nonjudgmental suggestions, and consistent encouragement greatly increases your likelihood of success.

So, who are the supportive people in your life?

_____

_____

_____

© JIST Works

Starting a business is a major life change, and even though the change is positive, it *will be stressful*. You also are creating major changes for your family, and their fears and concerns may make it difficult for them to be supportive right now. Don't be discouraged: Later, these same family members will be able to celebrate your successes with you. In the meantime, look for other sources of support among your network of extended family, friends, and business associates.

Summing Up

The first step in developing a clear mental image of your business is to consider your gifts, talents, and interests. We hope you are convinced of the importance of your daydreams. Communicate your business idea to people and identify friends or family who will be supportive. In the next chapter, we look at the next step toward making your dreams come true: How will you be able to finance your dreams?

CHAPTER 3

Financing the Dream

Financing your business can be a difficult task. Before you approach a lender or investor, it's important to understand the lending process and to be well prepared.

In this chapter, you learn the language of finance and read about the Four Ps of Finance and Five Cs of Lending. You also look at your credit options and what you need to do to finance your dream.

A Look at Your Business

1. Do you personally have enough money to finance your business dream?

   Yes_____ No_____

   If you checked No, answer the questions below.

2. How much money (in cash, equipment, and inventory) can you invest in your business?

   _____

3. Do family or friends have money they are willing to invest in your business?

   Yes_____ No_____ If so, how much? _____

4. If you and your family and friends cannot invest enough, how much money do you need to borrow to start a new business or maintain your existing business?

   _____

5. Write down how you would use invested or borrowed money in your business:

Amount	Purpose
$ _____	_____
$ _____	_____
$ _____	_____
$ _____	_____
$ _____	_____
$ _____	_____
$ _____	_____

6. Where can you go to borrow this money?

Financing 101

The dream of being self-employed is an exciting one, but a common obstacle to realizing that dream is a lack of money. Even if you succeed in starting a business, getting a loan to maintain or grow it is often difficult.

Before you seek money for your business dream, you should understand the basics of financing. In the rest of the chapter, we look at what a lender considers when reviewing a loan request, some common financial terms, how to identify essential business needs, how to create a financial plan, and why it's important to develop a relationship with your lender. We also review the loan application process, personal credit reports, and what you can expect if your loan request is approved.

The Risky Start-Up

Financing a business start-up is the riskiest loan a lender can make. A start-up business doesn't exist, so the owner cannot demonstrate its capacity to make a profit (and repay the loan). Even if the entrepreneur has significant experience producing the same product or service, being a successful entrepreneur requires a different set of skills.

For example, entrepreneurs must market and sell their products or services. They must manage cash flow daily, keep accurate records, understand financial reports, and use the reports to make informed decisions. They must set prices that are not too high or too low. Entrepreneurs must relate well to customers, employees, suppliers, and creditors. In time, successful entrepreneurs develop strong business management skills, but often, mistakes are made along the way. The magnitude of those mistakes can mean the difference between success and failure.

The business owner stands to benefit the most from (and has the most control over) a business success. Because of this, the owner is expected to assume the most risk when starting a business. Start-up businesses usually are financed through the personal resources of the business owner: savings, investments, equity in a home, and loans or investments from family and friends.

Sometimes, the entrepreneur must find a lender willing to finance the start-up. That lender is taking a chance on the unproven abilities of the entrepreneur, often a person not well known to the lender. It is in the best interests of the entrepreneur to develop an honest relationship with the lender. The entrepreneur must provide sufficient convincing information that the business start-up represents a worthy risk. The lender has to believe in the business idea and trust the entrepreneur. That trust must be earned, and building trust takes time.

The Existing Business

Is it any easier to get credit after a business owner has gathered enough resources to start a small business? The answer depends on a number of factors: the owner's relationship with the lender, the financial strength of the business, the way the owner manages the business, the borrower's ability to repay the loan, and the existence of an alternative method of repaying the loan if the business isn't as profitable as the owner projected.

Sometimes, a business owner approaches a lender only after the business is in financial crisis. The owner then is desperately seeking cash as a short-term solution to a significant problem, often with no long-range plans to keep the problem from reoccurring. This owner is unlikely to get a loan. Lenders prefer to develop long-term relationships with business owners who take the time—and have the ability—to manage their businesses well.

A borrower needs a clear idea of how much money the business needs and how the money will be used to maintain the business. If the business owner cannot explain these things clearly to the lender, the loan request likely will be denied. A lender is looking for a clear plan that explains how the money being borrowed will be invested to strengthen the business, or in other words, how the loan will help the business generate the additional income required to repay the loan.

It is important to prove that the business is borrowing enough money but not too much money. For example, a business may need money to buy equipment that will significantly increase its capacity to produce a product. With proper planning, increased production should result in increased sales. If the owner borrows too little, the equipment cannot be purchased. The borrowed money might be spent on operating costs until the funds are depleted. In the end, the business is left with no increase in sales and a debt it cannot repay.

Likewise, a business that borrows too much money may not increase its sales enough to generate the cash required to repay the loan. The key to determining how much money your business should borrow is proper planning.

Before turning to the steps of financing a business, take a look at some common financial terms.

The Language of Finance

- **Capital** is the money, equipment, or other major contribution invested to start a business. Capital typically is not recovered until a business is sold. Capital usually comes from two sources: investors (including the business owner) and lenders.

  - **Equity capital** is money the business owner or other people invest. Equity capital carries with it a share of ownership and, usually, a share in the profits.

  - **Debt capital** is money an owner borrows to start a business. This money must be repaid to the lender with interest.

- **Equity (or net worth)** is what remains when everything a company owes (its *liabilities*) is subtracted from everything a company owns (its *assets*). Equity can be greater than or less than the amount of capital invested in the business.

- **Collateral** is something of value the borrower owns and is willing to pledge as a secondary method of repayment if he or she fails to repay the loan in cash. The lender *secures* (lays claim to) the collateral at the time the loan is made so that no other lender can secure the same collateral during the life of the loan.

- A **loan** is money that is borrowed and must be repaid, usually under specified terms and conditions. There are three common types of loans:

  - **Short-term loans** provide money for short periods of time, usually 30 to 90 days. The original amount you borrow and must repay is called the *principal.* The fee charged for borrowing the money is called *interest.* In a short-term note, the money is used for the term of the note; then principal plus interest is repaid all at once.

  - A **line of credit** is an approved amount of money a borrower can access as needed. The repayment on a line of credit is established at the beginning of the loan. Repayment terms are flexible and may include monthly interest-only payments and quarterly or annual principal repayments.

  - **Long-term loans** often are used to buy real estate or equipment, and the purchased item is secured for *collateral.* (That is, the lender retains ownership of the real estate or the equipment until the loan is paid back.) Long-term loans have repayment terms of more than 12 months. Monthly payments are made, with a portion applied to interest and the remainder applied to the principal.

- **Working capital** is the amount of money available to pay short-term expenses. It's like a cushion to meet unexpected or out-of-the-ordinary expenses. A working capital loan can help a start-up business pay operating expenses for a short time as the business becomes self-sustaining. To get this kind of loan, a financial plan must show a business's ability to reach sustainability in a reasonable period of time.

Getting a Loan

The seven steps in this section help you go through the process of obtaining a loan to finance your business.

Identify Your Needs

The first step in financing your business is to identify your needs. Don't think in terms of dollars; think in terms of what your business needs. Do you need to buy equipment or inventory? Are you looking for a way to test your market?

When you have a list of your needs, examine it carefully and ask yourself this question: Is everything on the list essential? To determine the answer, identify those items that will generate money for your business and those that won't. Say, for example, you own an alterations business and you need a new sewing machine. Clearly, the sewing machine will generate income for your business: It's essential. A cellular phone might be convenient and a new desk might be nice, but they won't generate income for your business: They are not essential.

Use your judgment to separate essential and nonessential items. You might be able to operate your business inexpensively from your home. But if your customers expect your business to be located in an office or storefront, then renting space might be the only way to succeed.

After you have listed your essential needs, it's time to calculate their cost. You must request a loan amount that finances essential items and makes sense for your business. Don't begin the financing process with a dollar amount in mind. And don't base your request on how much you think you can borrow.

Develop a Financial Plan

The next step is creating a financial plan. Your plan will show the loan money coming into your business and your "essential needs" purchases being made. It will show money coming in from sales and money going out to pay expenses. Of course, it will show your business repaying the loan over a specific period of time. There are a few things a lender will want to see in your plan:

- **The projections must seem reasonable.** If you are financing a start-up business and you project high sales from the first day, your projections may not be realistic. In most businesses, sales start slowly and increase over time.

- **If your business will have seasonal fluctuations, these should be reflected in the plan.** A business that sells Christmas trees may have sales in November and December and none the rest of the year.

- **Finally, your operating expenses and the salary you take out must relate to the scale of your business.**

In Exercise #1, you will review two financial plans prepared for Dave's Lawn-Mowing Service. Try to think like a loan officer. Which plan seems like the best bet for your financial institution?

Exercise #1

Dave wants to borrow $2,000 to start a lawn-mowing service. He plans to start the business in January, operate the business part time, and have no employees. Review Dave's first financial plan below and then answer the questions that follow.

Dave's Lawn-Mowing Service

Six-Month Financial Plan #1
Loan Request: $2,000
Business Start-Up Date: January 1

Cash In	Start-Up	Jan	Feb	Mar	Apr	May	Jun	Total
Loan proceeds	$2,000							$2,000
Lawn-mowing income		$1,500	$1,500	$1,500	$1,500	$1,500	$1,500	$9,000
Total Cash In	$2,000	$1,500	$1,500	$1,500	$1,500	$1,500	$1,500	$11,000
Cash Out								
Lawn mower	$1,500							$1,500
Gas & oil for mower		$350	$350	$350	$350	$350	$350	$2,100
Truck expenses		$250	$250	$250	$250	$250	$250	$1,500
Advertising		$100	$100	$100	$100	$100	$100	$600
Insurance		$25	$25	$25	$25	$25	$25	$150
Loan payments		$0	$175	$175	$175	$175	$175	$875
Owner's salary	$500	$775	$600	$600	$600	$600	$600	$4,275
Total Cash Out	$2,000	$1,500	$1,500	$1,500	$1,500	$1,500	$1,500	$11,000
Remaining Cash Balance	**$0**	**$0**	**$0**	**$0**	**$0**	**$0**	**$0**	**$0**

1. Does Dave's plan seem realistic? Yes_____ No_____ Why? _____

_____

_____

2. How does Dave plan to use the loan money?_____

3. Does Dave include a plan to repay the loan? Yes_____ No_____

4. Do Dave's sales projections seem reasonable? Yes_____ No_____

   Is his salary reasonable? Yes_____ No_____

   Do his expenses seem reasonable? Yes_____ No_____

5. How could Dave improve this financial plan?_____

_____

6. Based on this financial plan, would you loan Dave the $2,000 he is requesting?

   Yes_____ No_____

© JIST Works

Dave has revised his business idea. Notice that in his revised plan, Dave has decided to wait until April 1 to start his new business. Review Dave's revised plan below and then answer the questions that follow.

Dave's Lawn-Mowing Service

Six-Month Financial Plan #2
Loan Request: $2,000
Business Start-Up Date: April 1

Cash In	Start-Up	Apr	May	Jun	Jul	Aug	Sep	Total
Loan proceeds	$2,000							$2,000
Lawn-mowing income		$350	$450	$550	$650	$800	$800	$3,600
Total Cash In	$2,000	$350	$450	$550	$650	$800	$800	$5,600
Cash Out								
Lawn mower	$1,500							$1,500
Gas & oil for mower		$35	$45	$55	$65	$80	$80	$360
Truck expenses		$53	$67	$83	$97	$120	$120	$540
Advertising		$50	$50	$50	$50	$50	$25	$275
Insurance		$25	$25	$25	$25	$25	$25	$150
Loan payments		$175	$175	$175	$175	$175	$175	$1,050
Owner's salary	$0	$50	$100	$150	$200	$325	$400	$1,225
Total Cash Out	$1,500	$388	$462	$538	$612	$775	$825	$5,100
Remaining Cash Balance	**$500**	**$462**	**$450**	**$462**	**$500**	**$525**	**$500**	**$500**

1. Does this plan seem more reasonable than the first? Yes_____ No_____ Why?_____

_____

_____

2. How does Dave plan to use the loan money?_____

3. Does Dave include a plan to repay the loan? Yes_____ No_____

4. Do Dave's sales projections seem reasonable? Yes_____ No_____

   Is his salary reasonable? Yes_____ No_____

   Do his expenses seem reasonable? Yes_____ No_____

5. How could Dave improve this financial plan?_____

_____

6. Based on this financial plan, would you loan Dave the $2,000 he is requesting?

   Yes_____ No_____

The Application Process

Loan application requirements vary among lenders. You probably will be required to submit a business plan (or at least an executive summary) that describes the products or services you will sell, short- and long-term goals for your business, information about you and your management staff, your marketing strategy, and financial information.

When you are using your business plan to get financing, you should include a specific financing request. The financing request, or *use of funds statement,* is simply a breakdown of how you propose to use the loan. The use of funds statement should be as detailed as possible, including equipment, model numbers, descriptions, and prices. Include catalogs or brochures describing the equipment you want to buy. Remember that your use of funds statement must be supported by the financial plan you submit. Here is an example of a use of funds statement:

Use of Funds Statement

Equipment: High-speed Laser Printer Model 5400 (see brochure attached) — $1,000
Advertising: Town Crier Newspaper, ½" display ads for 4 weeks
Radio advertising 30-second spots (see details attached) — $500
Working Capital — $1,000
Total Loan Request — **$2,500**

Your lender probably has a loan application packet. Pick up the packet and take it home with you. Fill it out neatly and completely. Don't forget to attach any additional information the lender requests, such as personal financial statements or tax returns. *If you have questions, ask them.* If you or your business have issues that may be of concern to your lender, don't try to hide them: Bring them up when you make your loan request and address them honestly.

The Five Cs of Lending

Following are the Five Cs of lending, which are considerations a loan officer makes while reviewing your credit application. Be prepared to answer questions and provide information about these five Cs:

- **Good Character:** The owner's personal integrity
- **Capacity:** The company's financial strength and ability to repay its debt
- **Capital:** How much debt the company has compared to its equity
- **Collateral:** A secondary source of repayment
- **Conditions:** The conditions of the economy and the industry

© JIST Works

Get to Know Your Lender

While you are in the early stages of identifying your needs and creating your financial plan, begin establishing a relationship with your lender. Stop in and say hello. Introduce yourself. Tell the lender you are in the planning stages of financing a business. Don't take a lot of his or her time talking about your business idea before you're ready to make your loan request. Simply let the lender know who you are and that you intend to approach him or her when you are ready.

The Four Ps of Finance

- **Preparation:** Be thorough when you prepare your business plan, and be prepared when you approach lenders and investors.

- **Presentation:** You must be ready and able to sell yourself and your business to others. Practice with friends before you approach lenders and investors.

- **Positive attitude:** You must project confidence in yourself and in your business. A positive attitude comes from thorough preparation, practice, and a strong belief in your ability to succeed.

- **Persistence:** This might be the most important ingredient in getting financing. Prepare to be turned down several times before you succeed. If you are turned down, ask yourself some questions: How can I make this work? What can I change to get the financing I need? Finding money is not always easy, but it is possible!

It's also a good idea to do your personal banking at the institution where you plan to request your loan. If you have a separate business checking account, some banks require that you have it there. And don't do your banking at the drive-through window. Go into the office, stop by the loan officer's desk, and say hello.

Remember, business is about relationships. People do business with people they know and like. Whether yours is a start-up or an existing business, begin a relationship with the lender well before you need a loan. After all, you'll be asking the lender to share a financial risk with you, and your working relationship will last a long time. So let the loan officer get to know you. Be a familiar face!

Personal Credit

Someone has been watching you! Each time you've signed for a car loan, used a credit card, or taken out a mortgage, the activity has been reported to a credit bureau. If you have a history of making late payments, it shows up on your personal credit report. If you have failed to repay a loan as promised, had a court judgment against you, had any tax liens filed against you, or filed personal bankruptcy within the last 10 years, it shows up on your credit report. But there's good news, as well: If you have made your payments on time, repaid your debts as promised, and have a track record of being a reliable credit risk, that shows up on your credit report, too!

Most applications for personal credit require you to sign a form that allows the creditor to obtain a copy of your personal credit report. Likewise, when you request financing for your business, lenders will require you to sign forms that allow them to obtain your personal credit report. Your personal credit is a major consideration, even when you are applying for a business loan. (Your lender is taking a risk on you as well as your business.) Your credit report tells a story about you, and you should know what the story is before you apply for a loan.

Order your own credit report at least once a year, and check it for accuracy. Sometimes credit bureaus make mistakes, and other people's credit transactions can show up on your report. You can ask a credit bureau to correct errors on your report by filing the appropriate paperwork. Be prepared to prove your claims. If you have difficulty getting a credit bureau to remove an item from your report, you can at least have them note that the entry is in dispute. If you are (or were) married and you and your spouse have (or had) joint accounts, each of your credit reports will include those accounts.

Your report may show a poor credit history at a time when you experienced some hardship, such as a divorce or a medical catastrophe. You probably can address this on your credit report. Most credit bureaus allow you to submit a short narrative explaining the circumstances of poor or questionable credit. This narrative will appear when a creditor requests a copy of your credit history. Many lenders are willing to take hardships into consideration when reviewing your credit. You must address these issues with your lenders: Tell them what they will find before they find it, and be honest.

If your report reflects a recent or current period of poor or no repayment, your lender will look for indications that you are trying to rebuild your credit. There are several ways to do this. One of the best is to get help from a nonprofit consumer credit counseling agency. These agencies help you get copies of your credit history, correct reporting errors, and establish a plan to rebuild your credit.

You've Been Approved! Now What?

If your loan request is approved, your lender may write a commitment letter that outlines the terms and conditions of the loan. Lenders are required by law to state clearly the interest rate charged on a loan: This is called the Annual Percentage Rate (APR). Your lender will schedule a loan closing, at which time you will sign the documents required by the lender and receive your loan proceeds. Typical loan documents include these:

- **A promissory note:** When you sign this note, you promise to repay the loan under the specified terms.
- **A security agreement:** By signing this, you give the lender a secured interest in the collateral you have pledged.
- **A personal guaranty:** Lenders usually require the owner(s) of a business to personally guarantee the loan. This means that if the business is unable to repay the loan for any reason, the owner(s) agree to assume personal responsibility for repayment.

Read all the loan documents carefully, and ask questions about anything you don't understand before you sign anything.

Your lender may charge closing fees to help cover the administrative costs of the loan. Ask about closing fees before the closing. Fees can be paid by the borrower at the closing, deducted from the loan proceeds, or added to the balance of the loan.

© JIST Works

An Interest in You!

Lenders are businesses, and they cover their operating and administrative expenses by charging interest on loans. *Interest* is the fee the borrower pays in exchange for access to credit. Interest typically is charged according to an annual percentage rate (APR): If your annual interest rate is 12 percent, you will be charged 1 percent interest (one-twelfth) on the balance of your loan each month. Below is an amortization schedule that shows the principal and interest breakdown of each monthly payment. Your lender can explain how interest and principal are calculated on your loan.

Amortization Schedule

Loan Date: 26-Jan-2XXX
Amount: $2,000.00
Interest Rate: 12.00%
Term: 24 months
Payment Amount: $94.15

Payment #	Due Date	Beg Bal	Amt Paid	Interest	Principal	Ending Bal
1	01-Mar	$2,000.00	$94.15	$20.00	$74.15	$1,925.85
2	01-Apr	$1,925.85	$94.15	$19.26	$74.89	$1,850.96
3	01-May	$1,850.96	$94.15	$18.51	$75.64	$1,775.32
4	01-Jun	$1,775.32	$94.15	$17.75	$76.39	$1,698.93
5	01-Jul	$1,698.93	$94.15	$16.99	$77.16	$1,621.77
6	01-Aug	$1,621.77	$94.15	$16.22	$77.93	$1,543.84
7	01-Sep	$1,543.84	$94.15	$15.44	$78.71	$1,465.13
8	01-Oct	$1,465.13	$94.15	$14.65	$79.50	$1,385.63
9	01-Nov	$1,385.63	$94.15	$13.86	$80.29	$1,305.34
10	01-Dec	$1,305.34	$94.15	$13.05	$81.09	$1,224.25
11	01-Jan	$1,224.25	$94.15	$12.24	$81.90	$1,142.35
12	01-Feb	$1,142.35	$94.15	$11.42	$82.72	$1,059.63
13	01-Mar	$1,059.63	$94.15	$10.60	$83.55	$976.08
14	01-Apr	$967.08	$94.15	$9.76	$84.39	$891.69
15	01-May	$891.69	$94.15	$8.92	$85.23	$806.46
16	01-Jun	$806.46	$94.15	$8.06	$86.08	$720.38
17	01-Jul	$720.38	$94.15	$7.20	$86.94	$633.44
18	01-Aug	$633.44	$94.15	$6.33	$87.81	$545.63
19	01-Sep	$545.63	$94.15	$5.46	$88.69	$456.94
20	01-Oct	$456.94	$94.15	$4.57	$89.58	$367.36
21	01-Nov	$367.36	$94.15	$3.67	$90.47	$276.89
22	01-Dec	$276.89	$94.15	$2.77	$91.38	$185.51
23	01-Jan	$185.51	$94.15	$1.86	$92.29	$93.22
24	01-Feb	$93.22	$94.15	$0.93	$93.22	($0.00)
Total:		**$2,000.00**	**$2,259.53**	**$259.53**	**$2,000.00**	**($0.00)**

Ending Bal = Beg Bal – Principal

Summing Up

Making small business loans is a risky proposition for lenders. When you apply for a small business loan, be prepared to answer questions and make a strong argument that you and your business have the ability to repay the loan. To be adequately prepared, you should

- Identify the essential items you need to start, strengthen, or grow your business.
- Create a realistic financial plan that demonstrates how the loan proceeds will be used and how your business will repay the loan.
- Include all the essential information the lender will need to make a decision, such as a detailed use of funds statement and the manufacturer's information about any equipment you propose to buy.
- Be aware of what your personal credit history says about you. If there are errors on your credit report, correct them before applying for your loan. If there are issues that require an explanation, be prepared to honestly address them with your lender.

CHAPTER 4

The Goal Train

For some people, life goes around and around like a train on a circular track. They work, pay bills, and deal with family and friends day after day, year after year, around and around. In this chapter, we look at how you can throw the switch on the tracks so you can go new places and accomplish new things.

We have all made things happen in our lives, like graduating from high school or college, losing weight, paying off bills, learning to dance, or taking a trip. Think of something you have accomplished that took some time, effort, and maybe money.

What was your accomplishment?_____

_____

_____

What steps did you take to achieve your accomplishment? _____

_____

_____

_____

On Your Mark, Get Set, Goal!

Most people would agree that setting goals is an important step in fulfilling dreams, yet only 5 percent of Americans actually write down their life goals and monitor them. The process of setting goals is not complicated, but it does require you to be honest with yourself and do some serious thinking about what you really want to achieve.

Keep in mind that successful people do set goals, and they use these goals to make decisions and keep themselves focused. Setting goals is an important step in achieving what you want from life, so in this chapter we go through the process of naming your goals and then using them to stay focused on what you really want from life.

In Chapter 2, we discussed how every business begins with a dream. In this chapter, we look at the ten steps to taking control of our lives and sending our train of life along different tracks.

Here's a brief look at the ten steps before we go into detail:

1. **Know yourself.** Knowing who you are gives you a sense of direction. Take time to inventory your strengths and weaknesses.

2. **Define your values.** Your values are what you believe in and what you would like to represent. They determine how you treat people, the relationships you seek, and your ideas of right and wrong. Values are your fundamental convictions.

3. **Research your choices.** Based on your personal inventory and your value system, list all of the business possibilities that could work for you. Read business books and magazines and talk to business owners about their businesses.

4. **Establish your goals.** Write goal statements that are achievable and measurable.

5. **Create an action plan.** Base your plan on the information you have about yourself, your values, and your goals. List the steps you need to take and the resources (money and time) required to accomplish your goals. Prioritize the steps. Ask yourself a couple of questions: Are these goals realistic? Do you have the necessary resources available to implement your plan?

> *A goal is a dream with a deadline!*

6. **Examine your motivation.** Positive motivation excites, energizes, and generates excellence. Motivation is a key ingredient of success.

7. **Learn discipline.** Successful people do not succumb to procrastination or temporary setbacks. They overcome obstacles with an inner strength: discipline. You can learn to be disciplined. The more disciplined you become, the more control you will have over your life.

8. **Be flexible.** Be ready to constantly reevaluate yourself, your values, your goals, and your action plan. Be ready to modify your strategies when change occurs, because it will.

9. **Make a decision.** At some point, you will have all of the information you need to decide whether to start a particular business or not. If the decision is to move forward, then make that part of your action plan. It is also okay to decide not to proceed with a business idea. In fact, that's the whole idea of researching—to determine if a business will work for you or not. Your research costs you time but is well worth it.

10. **Reach an outcome.** The outcome is the destination of your journey. When you arrive, take time to evaluate your trip. Did you accomplish what you set out to accomplish? What did you learn along the way? Get ready to set your next goals.

In the following pages, we look at each of these steps in more detail.

Know Yourself

Who are you? Explain yourself in terms of your attitudes and your self-image. What do others think of you? What do you do well? What tasks are you uncomfortable doing? What are your weaknesses? Try not to define yourself in terms of what you own or in terms of "shoulds," and don't define yourself in terms of the roles you play (mother, husband, daughter, etc.).

© JIST Works

In the space below, write a short description of who you are. Be honest. This inventory may be uncomfortable, but it is necessary if you want to improve yourself or make decisions about your new business.

_____

_____

_____

Define Your Values

Have you ever dreamed for months about going on a great vacation and then had that vacation be a miserable experience? The same thing can happen if the decisions in your life are not based on sound values. The outcome may leave you feeling dissatisfied and empty.

Values—also called principles, ideals, purposes, beliefs, and convictions—are your most important fundamental beliefs.

Suppose your goal was to win a race, but in order to win, you tripped your opponent. Would the outcome leave you feeling triumphant? Probably not.

How you play is based on your values, and this holds true in business, too.

- What values do you want to instill in your children?

_____

_____

_____

- What three values would you want people to identify with you?

_____

_____

_____

Research Your Choices

Lots of business opportunities are available, but some of them will not fit your personality or value system. Begin by considering any business that is interesting to you. List the pros and cons of that business. Find business owners who are willing to talk with you about what being in that business is like. Get educated about the issues that are related to your business of interest. Look at practical things like the amount of money it would take to start the business, the amount of money you could make, the hours that would be involved, the type of customers you would deal with, and the type of work involved.

Establish Your Goals

Any farmer can tell you that when you plow a field, you must keep your eyes fixed on one point on the horizon. Without that fixed point, your row will meander all over the field. The same is true in life. If you don't keep a specific target in sight, you'll wander off course.

Your goals must be specific. It's not enough to simply say that you want to be happy, or be successful, or be wealthy, or travel. Your goals also should be measurable; they should have a time frame as well as an intended result. If you don't clearly define both a time and an intended result, how will you know when you've reached the goal?

Goals should answer the following questions:

- Where am I going?
- How am I going to get there?
- How much will it cost me to get there?
- How long will it take me to get there?
- How will I know when I have arrived?

Your goals should be challenging but realistic. Set goals you think you can reach: It's better to up your goals later than to set them so high that you give up. Setting goals that are unreasonable is self-defeating; they'll only keep you from succeeding.

> *Remember, your goals and business objectives must be in agreement with your basic values.*

Visualize your goals. When you begin to see a dream, you can make it happen. After you've visualized them, write your goals down, keeping in mind that a list of goals is more than a list of chores.

Reward yourself when you reach your goal. Reward yourself for the great effort you put in, even if the goal did not turn out completely as expected.

Create an Action Plan

An old Chinese proverb applies here: The journey of 10,000 miles starts with a single step. Focusing only on the end result doesn't get you where you need to be today or tomorrow. It only overwhelms you.

You must determine what steps you need to take today to reach your outcome. Planning brings the future into the present so you can do something about it. What needs to be done to make your dream a reality? Where do you start? What strategy will work best? What resources will give you the outcome you want?

At the end of this chapter, you will find goal activity pages on which to record your goals, the steps to reach them, your target dates, the person responsible, the money and time required, and the results.

> *Action cures fear.*

When you have finished reading, write your goals, list the steps, prioritize them, and begin! Don't wait until the conditions are perfect. Expect problems, and tackle each one as soon as you encounter it.

If you are afraid of taking action, don't look at all the steps ahead of you. Concentrate on one step at a time. Focus just on what is required to complete that single step. Then do it!

© JIST Works

Examine Your Motivation

Before we discuss motivation, consider a symbol of business prosperity—the frog! The frog is a symbol of business prosperity because it can only move forward. The frog is incapable of moving backward or sideways. And, as one of our students pointed out, sometimes the frog sits still for a very long time, but when the frog moves, it only moves forward.

To be successful in your own business, you must make things happen. You are the only one who can build the bridge between thinking about your goals and accomplishing them. Self-motivation is the driving force behind high achievement. It's the inner desire that keeps you always moving forward in spite of discouragement, mistakes, and setbacks. There are several steps to self-motivation, including these:

- **Believe in yourself.** Make success and happiness part of your self-image.
- **Think only positive thoughts.**
- **Welcome challenges.**
- **Be flexible to change.**
- **Take pride in your achievements.**
- **Set goals that are stimulating, challenging, and achievable.**
- **Overcome fear.** Fear is the opposite of desire. It creates stress, panic, and anxiety and defeats plans and goals. To overcome fear, you must understand where it's coming from. Then take action; action cures fear.
- **Start now.** Don't wait until you have all the information or the circumstances are perfect. Begin now. Get in motion as soon as possible. As your momentum builds, so will your motivation.
- **Focus on the rewards.** Visualize the rewards of success in your mind as clearly and vividly as you can.

Learn Discipline

Being disciplined means sticking to an action plan even when there are other things you'd rather do. It is hard work. It takes guts. It means staying focused and practicing better work habits.

Being disciplined means taking responsibility for yourself. Many people are quite good at blaming others for their own shortcomings. It's easy to blame outside forces for failure. But if you are going to be a successful entrepreneur, you must stop making excuses and take charge of your own life and your own success.

You may need to start small. Take control of your day today. This is the first step in taking control of your success.

Be Flexible

Change is constant; you cannot avoid it. Try to see change as an opportunity instead of as a problem. Change is growth: It can improve your life if you let it. Accept change in your life as normal and positive. Don't just stand there, change!

Make a Decision

By taking the time to look at yourself and to examine different businesses, you will decide to move forward with a business idea or decide not to start that particular business. If you've done your homework, you should feel good about making a decision based on facts.

Reach an Outcome

Whatever the outcome of your goal, hold it in high regard. Focus on what you did right instead of what you did wrong. Then set another goal.

If these ideas are new to you, read them again until you begin to believe them. Then, practice setting goals. Soon, you'll be convinced that it's the best way to take control of your life and your business.

> *Remember, your business goals must mesh with your personal goals and values if you are going to succeed!*

Three Scenarios

Meet Gail, Jerry, and Daryl. Each has a new business venture. Read the descriptions of their business ideas and the goals they have set for themselves. What do you predict will be the outcome for each? Why?

How to Make an American Quilt

Gail plans to make quilts at home and sell them on consignment through craft boutiques, home decorating stores, and the colonial village tourist site outside of town. She has received a loan of $1,200 to buy a cutting table, cutting tools, and an old sewing machine. Four stores have agreed to take a total of 10 quilts on consignment, and she has a good list of additional stores to contact.

Gail plans to spend about 25 hours a week sewing and 5 hours a week making new contacts. Each quilt takes about 15 hours to make.

Gail has set several goals for the next six months:

- To purchase a table, cutting tools, and supplies within the next month
- To start sewing by the end of the first month
- To average 1½ quilts per week and to deliver the 10 quilts that have already been accepted for consignment within the first two months

© *JIST Works*

- To sell eight quilts a month
- At the end of six months, to reevaluate goals and decide if there is enough business to invite a friend to work with her part time

Painting Himself into a Corner?

Jerry has been painting houses to earn money on the side, helping out a buddy with a painting business. Now Jerry has been laid off from his factory job, and he's decided to start painting full time. His buddy needs help sometimes, but he prefers to work alone when he can handle it, so Jerry has decided to start his own business. Jerry has no experience in soliciting jobs; he's just worked on them.

Jerry figures that to make it work, he has to meet these goals:

- Get an $8,000 loan to buy a used truck and the ladders and equipment he'll need before he can take any jobs
- Paint 50 hours a week and do publicity 10 hours a week
- Find a minimum of three jobs per month for the first three months
- By the end of three months, increase from three jobs to nine jobs per month and hire a helper

Jerry figures he can collect unemployment for the first three months, but after his unemployment runs out, he'll have to double his business. To handle that much work, he'll have to hire a helper, which means more expense. So he really needs to triple his business to make enough money to cover his bills and living expenses.

Hot Stuff or a Hot Spot?

Daryl makes a mean chili. His buddies have been telling him for years that he should sell the stuff. He has a job, which he'll keep, but he's decided to start his own business on the side. He's going to call it *Hot Stuff*.

Daryl got the idea for his business while he was at a concert in a downtown park. He saw several food concessions there selling mediocre food at high prices. Daryl figures he's got a better food product. There must be a way to make money charging the kind of prices he saw at the concert.

Daryl's got enough money put away to buy a small cart with a warming unit for about $800. He figures the first time there's a big concert downtown, he'll cook up a big batch of his best chili and head for the park. Hey, what does he have to lose?

Practice Writing Effective Goals

Effective goals should be realistic, be measurable, and state a target date. Rewrite the following statements so each becomes an effective goal.

Example: Increase sales by $3,000. Is this goal realistic? Is it measurable? Does it state a target date?

Change the goal to read:

In 2XXX, sales were $30,000. Increase sales by $3,000 (10 percent) for 2XXY. Now is the goal realistic? Is it measurable? Does it state a target date?

1. Triple total sales within three months. _____

_____

2. Hire new employees within a year._____

_____

3. Visit several other businesses to get new ideas. _____

_____

4. Grow from one site to three before Christmas. _____

_____

5. Improve publicity this year. _____

_____

6. Buy a new pickup by the time I start taking jobs. _____

_____

7. Within the next two months, visit community workers who could tell families about my child care service. _____

_____

8. Move work space out of my home. _____

_____

9. Set aside $500 to hire an artist to design packaging. _____

_____

© *JIST Works*

Write Your Own Goals

In the exercise that follows, you will write your own goals. State your goal, the action plan to reach the goal, the target date, the person responsible, the money and time required, and the results. After you write all your goals and action steps, prioritize them and *begin*. Consider asking someone on your support team (see Chapter 2) to review your plan. Take a look at the following example of a plan written by a person who wants to start a child care business in her home.

Goal/Action Plan

My ultimate goal is: To open a child care business in my home

This is my ultimate target date: September 2XXX

Here are the steps I will take to reach my goal, along with the target date for each:

1. Write a business plan—June 2XXX

2. Prepare my home for the business—July 2XXX

3. Complete the child care paperwork required by my state—July 2XXX

4. Find five customers—August 2XXX

The person responsible for each step is:

1. Me

2. Me

3. Me

4. Me

The money and time requirements are:

1. Business plan. No cost, only time—5 hours a week for 6 weeks

2. Paint the two rooms I will use for the child care business and find the equipment I need. $450 and 3 hours over 4 weekends.

3. Complete the paperwork. $150 for the state licenses and 5 hours—3 hours to research what I need and 2 hours to complete and return the information.

4. Find five customers. $5 for copies and 4 hours—1 hour to write a short ad for my church bulletin, 1 hour to create a flyer, and 2 hours to deliver copies of the flyer to my neighbors and friends and place them on the bulletin boards of the two grocery stores that are in my neighborhood.

Here are the results:

My business plan was completed on May 15, 2XXX.

The two rooms were painted by July 2XXX. I found all of the equipment I needed by the end of July 2XXX.

The child care paperwork was completed on August 1, 2XXX.

I found my first five customers by August 15, 2XXX.

My child care business is ready to open on September 1, 2XXX!

Goal/Action Plan

My ultimate goal is: _____

_____

_____

This is my ultimate target date: _____

Here are the steps I will take to reach my goal, along with the target date for each:

1. _____

2. _____

3. _____

4. _____

The person responsible for each step is:

1. _____

2. _____

3. _____

4. _____

The money and time requirements are: _____

_____

_____

Here are the results: _____

_____

_____

Goal/Action Plan

My ultimate goal is: _____

_____

_____

This is my ultimate target date: _____

Here are the steps I will take to reach my goal, along with the target date for each:

1. _____

2. _____

3. _____

4. _____

© JIST Works

The person responsible for each step is:

1. _____

2. _____

3. _____

4. _____

The money and time requirements are: _____

_____

_____

Here are the results: _____

_____

_____

Summing Up

Remember, successful people set goals. If you want to go to new places and accomplish new things, begin to know your strengths and weaknesses. Take time to examine your values so you can establish goals that will draw you where you want to go. Don't forget to create an Action Plan that lists the steps and the time and money required to accomplish each step. In the next chapter, we discuss how to price your products and services to make a profit.

CHAPTER 5

Pricing Your Products and Services

Proper pricing can mean the difference between success and failure in your business. When businesses don't take the time to examine their price structures, they may find (often too late) that they have not priced their products or services properly.

Underpricing can cause a business to fail; if products are drastically underpriced, the business loses money every time a sale is made. Overpricing can cause sales to disappear altogether as customers buy from lower-priced competitors.

In this chapter, you learn about pricing products and services. You also learn how to perform a break-even analysis to determine if your price structure is sound.

1. Write down why you think proper pricing is important.

_____

_____

_____

_____

_____

2. Why do you believe business owners under- or overprice products or services?

_____

_____

_____

_____

3. List some of the consequences of underpricing.

_____

_____

_____

_____

_____

4. Why do you think business owners are unaware that their products are not properly priced?

_____

_____

_____

_____

_____

A business should have two aims in determining its pricing system: (1) to price its products or services competitively and (2) to ensure that all business expenses can be paid and a profit earned, given a reasonable level of sales. In order to make this happen, the business owner needs to answer the following questions:

- What prices are appropriate for my market?
- What are my business expenses?
- What are reasonable sales goals for my business?

In the following sections, we look at how you can answer each of these questions accurately so you can ensure proper pricing for your business.

What Price Is Right?

The real price of a product or service is no more than the customer is willing to pay. Finding out how much your customers are willing to pay requires some research on your part. Below are several sources of information on pricing. Use as many of them as you can to determine what prices are appropriate for your market.

Customer Surveys

One way to determine pricing is to survey your potential customers. This is possible only if you can easily identify and locate your potential customers, which is difficult for some businesses. It also may be a challenge to get an honest answer to the question, "How much would you be willing to pay for this?" Some businesses mail surveys to their target customers, and some survey individuals in public places.

Shopping Your Competition

Another way to find out what the market will bear is to "shop" the competition. If your competitors operate from retail stores, a quick trip to their shops allows you to see what they charge for similar products and services and whether they appear to be making sales. You can make phone calls to determine hourly rates commonly charged by service industry competitors. This way, you not only find out what your competitors charge, but you also get a good feel for their level of customer service. Shopping your competition allows you to experience whether your competitors are respectful to their customers, answer and return phone calls promptly, and are knowledgeable about their industry.

© JIST Works

Market Research Sales

Selling your goods or services at a marketplace or fair—or temporarily subleasing a small space in an existing shop—is an effective way to determine appropriate pricing, as well as help you determine if your business idea is feasible. This approach also gives you hands-on experience at operating your business. In order to use this approach, you will need a small supply of inventory. You should make certain you are not required to rent booth or floor space in a long-term lease. Remember, this is just an exercise in market research to help you determine how to price your products.

While you operate your temporary business, listen to what your customers tell you. If customers continually comment on how low your prices are, you may have some room to raise them. On the other hand, if your products create interest but no sales, you might consider lowering your prices.

What Are Your Expenses?

In order to operate a successful business, the pricing structure must take into account all of the expenses of running the business. Expenses must be identified and divided into two categories: cost of goods sold and fixed expenses.

Cost of Goods Sold

The direct expenses of creating your product or service are called the *cost of goods sold* (COGS). If your business sells wooden toys that are handcrafted and painted, then the wood, the paint, and the time it takes to make the toys are all COGS. If your business sells beaded jewelry, then all of the materials (beads, thread, glue, clasps, pins, etc.) plus the cost of labor (the time it takes to make each piece of jewelry) are the COGS. If you provide a service, such as a secretarial service, the COGS might include paper and file folders plus the cost of the labor. In a cleaning business, the COGS might include cleaning supplies, transportation costs for cleaning crews, and labor.

Fixed Expenses

Some expenses exist whether or not a business has any sales. These are called *fixed expenses*. Examples of typical fixed expenses include rent, insurance, utilities, legal and accounting costs, and advertising. Fixed expenses are usually recurring expenses for things that are consumed (or used up) during the course of normal operations. These expenses sometimes are referred to as *overhead expenses*. Fixed expenses do not substantially increase or decrease with changes in sales volume. Because of this, fixed expenses are easy to identify.

Capital Expenditures

There is a third type of expense: capital expenditures. Capital expenditures include the cost of purchasing nonrecurring major items for your business that are not consumed (used up) during normal business operations—for example, one-time purchases of land, buildings, furniture, or major equipment. Capital expenditures usually exceed a certain dollar amount (which varies from business to business) and increase the value of your business (your business is worth more if you sell it). Capital expenditures are not included in the break-even calculation or considered when pricing products. Business owners pay for capital expenditures out of net profit, and net profit is not generated until sales exceed the break-even point.

The Break-Even Analysis

After you identify your COGS and your fixed expenses, you can perform a *break-even analysis*. This tells you how many products or services you must sell at a given price in order to cover the expenses of your business. The *break-even point* is the point at which adequate sales are made to cover your business expenses, but before a profit is earned. It's important to perform this analysis because it allows you to determine if your price structure is sound. It will also give you minimal sales goals for your business.

Before we actually perform a break-even analysis, we need to define a few terms.

- **Gross income** is the amount of income a business earns before expenses are considered.
- **Gross profit** is what remains when you subtract the cost of goods sold from the gross income. Fixed expenses are paid from the gross profit.
- **Net profit** is what remains when you subtract the fixed expenses from the gross profit.

Typically, this is how the information is put together:

When Will You Break Even?

In order for your business to succeed, you must have sufficient gross income so that there is enough gross profit to pay all of your fixed expenses after you subtract your cost of goods sold. The break-even point defines the actual number of products or services you must sell at a certain price in order to achieve this. A new business performs a break-even analysis after assuming the following three things:

1. **Gross income (or price) per product or service.** At first, this number is an educated guess based on what you learned about the marketplace. The break-even analysis will confirm whether or not this price is sufficient.

2. **Cost of goods sold per product or service.** You find this number by researching the cost of creating the product or service.

3. **Fixed expenses of the business.** This information comes from researching the cost of operating the business.

ABC Widgets & Gadgets

Income

Sales/Widgets	$500.00
Sales/Gadgets	+$400.00
Gross Income	*$900.00*

Cost of Goods Sold

Materials	$250.00
Labor	+$350.00
Total COGS	*$600.00*

Gross Profit	*$300.00*

Fixed Expenses

Rent	$100.00
Utilities	+$ 35.00
Total Fixed Expenses	*$135.00*

Net Profit	**$165.00**

© *JIST Works*

After you gather this information, you can perform a break-even analysis using the following two-part formula:

$$\text{Gross income} - \text{cost of goods sold} = \text{gross profit}$$

$$\text{Fixed expenses} \div \text{gross profit} = \text{break-even point}$$

For example, if we assume the following about a widget business:

Gross income per widget =	$9
Cost of goods sold per widget =	$4
Fixed expenses per month =	$1,000

then we can perform the break-even analysis as follows:

Gross income	$9
– cost of goods sold	– $4
= gross profit	$5
Fixed expenses	$1,000
÷ gross profit	÷ $5
= break-even point	200

This business must sell 200 widgets per month at $9 per widget to break even.

Now go through the following example to see how Sarah Sue performs a break-even analysis for her new business.

Sarah Sue's Scenario

All of Sarah Sue's friends rave about her sandwiches (she makes them with her secret sandwich sauce). With a great deal of encouragement from her family and friends, Sarah Sue is thinking about opening her own sandwich shop. At this point, she is in the information-gathering stage.

Sarah Sue has learned that a local deli owner is about to retire, and she has talked with him about renting his storefront. (This will cost her $600 per month.) Sarah Sue also got information about the costs of utilities for the storefront (about $150 per month), telephone (about $100 per month), and business insurance ($25 per month).

Sarah Sue examined her personal situation and made a determination about how much money she needs to earn in order to meet her financial obligations ($2,000 per month).

Armed with this information, Sarah Sue came up with the following list of fixed expenses for Sarah Sue's Sandwich Shop:

Fixed Expenses

Rent	$600
Utilities	$150
Telephone	$100
Business insurance	$25
Owner's salary	$2,000
Miscellaneous	$50
Total fixed expenses:	$2,925

Next, Sarah Sue must calculate the cost of goods sold for her sandwiches. Since the ingredients for the sandwiches will vary by order, Sarah Sue decides to start with what she believes will be her most popular sandwich: turkey and Swiss cheese on whole wheat (known as the *Swiss Gobbler*). She calculates the cost of making this sandwich with everything on it, as this will represent the highest COGS. Having received a price sheet from her food supplier, Sarah Sue came up with these figures:

Supplier Price Sheet and Labor Costs	Sarah Estimates	Ingredients per *Swiss Gobbler*	COGS *Swiss Gobbler*
Turkey $3.00/lb.	10 slices/lb.	2 slices	$ .60
Bread $.75/loaf	30 slices/loaf	2 slices	$ .05
Swiss cheese $3.00/lb.	10 slices/lb.	2 slices	$ .60
Mayonnaise $2.00/jar	32 ounces/jar	1 ounce	$ .06
Mustard $1.00/jar	32 ounces/jar	1 ounce	$ .03
Tomatoes $ .50 ea.	8 slices/tomato	1 slice	$ .06
Lettuce $ .60/head	30 leaves/head	2 leaves	$ .04
Secret sauce $3.00/jar	32 ounces/jar	1 ounce	$ .09
Wax paper $ .03/sheet	precut sheets	1 sheet	$ .03
Labor $8.00/hr.	15 sandwiches/hr.	4 minutes	$ .53
Total COGS:			**$2.09**

Sarah Sue has determined that it will cost her $2.09 to create her most popular sandwich. She has shopped the competition and surveyed her friends, and she believes that a fair price for this sandwich will be $4.95. Given these assumptions, Sarah Sue calculates the following:

$$\text{Gross income - COGS} = \text{gross profit}$$
$$\$4.95 - \$2.09 = \$2.86$$

$$\text{Fixed expenses} \div \text{gross profit} = \text{break-even point}$$
$$\$2,925 \div \$2.86 = 1,023$$

Sarah Sue will have to sell 1,023 *Swiss Gobblers* (or similarly priced sandwiches) each month to break even. To break the calculation down further, if Sarah Sue is open for business 6 days a week, or about 25 days each month, she will need to sell about 41 sandwiches per day to break even. Now, she can ask herself if this seems like a reasonable goal.

$$1,023 \text{ sandwiches} \div 25 \text{ days a month} = 40.9 \text{ sandwiches a day}$$

Profit Through Product Mix

Sarah Sue did a break-even analysis for one sandwich, the *Swiss Gobbler,* but what if she sells many kinds of sandwiches? And what if she wants to sell other items, such as beverages, French fries, and chips? How do we perform a break-even analysis on a variety of products? When a business offers a variety of products for sale, that variety is known as the *product mix.*

To determine pricing for your business's product mix, perform a break-even analysis on each product you will sell, as Sarah Sue did for the *Swiss Gobbler.* When you complete these analyses, you can estimate how many of each product you will sell in a given period of time. Multiply the gross profit for each item by the number you think you will sell. Then add the total gross profits together. Does this total gross profit equal or come close to your fixed expenses? If not, keep playing with the numbers sold until you get a product mix that does come close. When you have estimates that you believe are reasonable and adequate to cover your fixed expenses, you will have the break-even point for your product mix.

When you are doing this, make some assumptions that make sense for your business. For example, Sarah Sue knows that she has to sell 1,023 *Swiss Gobblers* to break even. She believes all of her sandwiches will be similarly priced, but she also wants to sell other products, such as French fries and beverages. She must price these products so that she makes a gross profit on each. She may not sell a beverage each time she sells a sandwich, but she may sell one with 90 percent of her sandwich sales. She may not sell French fries with each sandwich, but she may sell them with 75 percent of her sandwich sales. If she can make these additional (or *ancillary*) product sales, then she can sell far fewer than 1,023 sandwiches and still achieve her break-even point. Why? Because with each additional product sale she makes, Sarah Sue has even more gross profit to offset the cost of her fixed expenses.

For example, if Sarah Sue sells regular-size beverages for $1.50 and her cost of goods sold is $.90, her gross profit on each beverage will be $.60. If she sells French fries for $1.25 and her cost of goods sold is $.35, then her gross profit on each sale is $.90. Sarah Sue may calculate the following:

Gross profit on sandwiches = $2.86

Gross profit on beverages = $ .60

    Beverages sold with 90 percent of sandwiches

    $ .60 x 90% = $ .54 gross profit per sandwich sale

Gross profit on French fries = $ .90

    French fries sold with 75 percent of the sandwiches

    $ .90 x 75% = $ .68 gross profit per sandwich sale

When she adds her gross profits together, she gets a gross profit for a product mix:

    $2.86 + $ .54 + $ .68 = $4.08

Sarah Sue now applies her break-even formula:

    Fixed expenses ÷ gross profit = break-even point

    $2,925 ÷ $4.08 = 717

Sarah Sue can sell 717 sandwiches and achieve her break-even point, as long as she also sells beverages 90 percent of the time (717 x 90% = 646 beverages) and French fries 75 percent of the time (717 x 75% = 538 orders of French fries). You can check your numbers by looking at them individually on this two-part worksheet:

Part 1

Gross income - COGS = gross profit

Sandwiches:	$4.95 - $2.09 = $2.86
Beverages:	$1.50 - $ .90 = $ .60
French fries:	$1.25 - $ .35 = $ .90

Part 2

Gross profit x # sold = total gross profit

$2.86 x 717 =	$2,051
$ .60 x 646 =	$ 388
$ .90 x 538 =	$ 484
Total Gross Profit:	$2,923
Total Fixed Expenses:	$2,925

This example illustrates why successful restaurants train their employees to ask, "Would you like fries with that?" each time they take an order. The difference between selling sandwiches alone (1,023 to break even) and selling sandwiches with a beverage and French fries (717 to break even) is dramatic.

If your business can't "group together" product sales, then simply make best-guess estimates of how many of each product you might sell and keep playing with the numbers until you get a gross profit that is adequate to cover your fixed expenses.

Work through the exercise below. Use the three worksheets provided. A second copy of each worksheet is provided for calculating a break-even analysis for your own business.

Mary's Lions, Tigers, and Bears

Mary is an artisan who makes unique creations from a studio in her home. She makes one-of-a-kind stuffed animals in three sizes: small (babies), large (adult animals), and giant (such as 6-foot-tall giraffes).

- A friend of Mary's has a shop in the village that sells hand-painted children's furniture and bedding. She has agreed to display Mary's stuffed animals in one corner of her shop for a flat fee of $300 per month.

- Mary also has a business phone line for which she pays $75 per month.

- She would like to be able to draw a salary of $1,000 per month, plus pay herself an hourly wage of $10 per hour to produce the stuffed animals.

- Mary sells her small stuffed animals for $35. Her materials costs average $5, and the small animals take Mary about 1 hour to make.

- Large animals sell for $50. Material costs average $7. They take about 1.5 hours to make.

- The giant animals sell for $150. Material costs are typically $30. Mary spends about 4 hours making a giant animal.

With the information provided above, work through Worksheets #1, #2, and #3. On Worksheet #1, determine what Mary's fixed expenses will be. On Worksheet #2, determine for each product or service what Mary's break-even points are. Finally, on Worksheet #3, finish the analysis with a reasonable product mix of services. Determine if Mary has a viable business idea.

© *JIST Works*

Tip: Include Mary's salary (also called *owner's compensation*) as a fixed expense. Include Mary's hourly labor cost per product as a cost of goods sold.

Owner's Compensation

What is the most common mistake small business owners make? Thinking their own labor is "free." If a business owner fails to include the cost of his or her time when calculating prices, the income will never be there to pay the owner. Smart business owners include the cost of their time in two places: in fixed expenses as a salary (this pays the owner for the administrative time it takes to manage the business) and in Cost of Goods Sold as an hourly wage (so the owner gets paid for the time spent producing products). Until sales reach the break-even point, you may choose not to take your salary or hourly wage out of the business, but at least it will be built into your pricing structure. Remember: If you make the mistake of believing your labor is "free," that is exactly what you will be paid!

Worksheet #1: Fixed Expenses

When identifying your monthly fixed expenses, use the average of what you expect your monthly expenses to be in the first six months. Include your target amount for owner's compensation. If you do not include your compensation in your pricing structure, you will never be able to afford to pay yourself this amount.

Fixed Expenses

Rent _____

Utilities _____

Telephone _____

Office supplies _____

Postage _____

Equipment repairs & maintenance _____

Insurance _____

Loan payments _____

Marketing costs _____

Subscriptions/Dues/Fees _____

Legal/Accounting _____

Owner's compensation _____

Other_____ _____

_____ _____

_____ _____

_____ _____

Total Monthly Fixed Expenses: _____

Worksheet #1: Fixed Expenses

When identifying your monthly fixed expenses, use the average of what you expect your monthly expenses to be in the first six months. Include your target amount for owner's compensation. If you do not include your compensation in your pricing structure, you will never be able to afford to pay yourself this amount.

Fixed Expenses

Rent _____

Utilities _____

Telephone _____

Office supplies _____

Postage _____

Equipment repairs & maintenance _____

Insurance _____

Loan payments _____

Marketing costs _____

Subscriptions/Dues/Fees _____

Legal/Accounting _____

Owner's compensation _____

Other_____ _____

_____ _____

_____ _____

_____ _____

_____ _____

Total Monthly Fixed Expenses: _____

© *JIST Works*

Worksheet #2: Pricing/Break-Even Analysis

Individual Products

Product Name: _____

Part 1   Gross Income   –   COGS   =   Gross Profit

Part 2   Fixed Expenses   ÷   Gross Profit   =   Break-Even

Product Name: _____

Part 1   Gross Income   –   COGS   =   Gross Profit

Part 2   Fixed Expenses   ÷   Gross Profit   =   Break-Even

Product Name: _____

Part 1   Gross Income   –   COGS   =   Gross Profit

Part 2   Fixed Expenses   ÷   Gross Profit   =   Break-Even

Worksheet #2: Pricing/Break-Even Analysis

Individual Products

Product Name: _____

Part 1   Gross Income   –   COGS   =   Gross Profit

Part 2   Fixed Expenses   ÷   Gross Profit   =   Break-Even

Product Name: _____

Part 1   Gross Income   –   COGS   =   Gross Profit

Part 2   Fixed Expenses   ÷   Gross Profit   =   Break-Even

Product Name: _____

Part 1   Gross Income   –   COGS   =   Gross Profit

Part 2   Fixed Expenses   ÷   Gross Profit   =   Break-Even

© JIST Works

Worksheet #3: Pricing/Break-Even Analysis

Product Mix

Part 1:	Income	–	COGS	=	Gross Profit
Product #1					
Product #2					
Product #3					
Product #4					
Total Fixed Expenses					$_____

Part 2:	Gross Profit	x	# sold	=	Total Gross Profit
Product #1					
Product #2					
Product #3					
Product #4					
Total Profits					
Total Fixed Expenses					$_____

Worksheet #3: Pricing/Break-Even Analysis

Product Mix

Part 1:	Income	–	COGS	=	Gross Profit
Product #1					
Product #2					
Product #3					
Product #4					
Total Fixed Expenses					$_____

(continued)

(continued)

Part 2:	Gross Profit	x	# sold	=	Total Gross Profit
Product #1					
Product #2					
Product #3					
Product #4					
Total Profits					
Total Fixed Expenses					$_____

Pricing for Service Providers

This formula (and the following worksheet) can be used to determine an appropriate hourly billing rate for a service provider. Service providers may include consultants, Web page designers, technicians, writers, and other small businesses that primarily sell their time.

Step 1. Determine your income requirements. Estimate your annual operating expenses (sometimes called overhead). These should include things like rent, utilities, insurance, and telephone service.

Next, decide how much personal income you need to earn. Don't forget to include the cost of self-employment tax, your estimated federal tax liability, and the cost of health insurance premiums.

Annual operating expenses:	$10,000
Owner's gross wages:	$30,000
Total income requirements:	$40,000

Step 2. Calculate available working hours. Multiply the number of weeks per year by the number of work hours per week.

52 weeks x 40 hours per week: 2,080 total hours

Subtract time off for annual vacations and holidays to get your total available work hours per year.

–40 vacation hours and 56 holiday hours: 2,080 – 96 = 1,984 available hours

Step 3. Estimate billable hours. Estimate what percentage of your available time you will be able to bill clients. Consider your expectations for gaining new jobs or new clients over time. This percentage may have seasonal fluctuations, depending on your business. Break down these estimates by months or quarters.

1,984 hours available per year

1,984 ÷ 4 = 496 hours available per quarter

	Available Hours	x	Percentage Billable Hours	=	Billable Hours per Quarter
Quarter 1:	496	x	20% (1 day per week)		99
Quarter 2:	496	x	25% (1 out of 4 days)		124
Quarter 3:	496	x	30% (1 out of 3 days)		149
Quarter 4:	496	x	40% (2 days per week)		198
Estimated Billable Hours:					570

Step 4. Calculate your hourly billing rate. Divide your total required income (from Step 1) by the number of estimated billable hours per year (from Step 3) to get your hourly rate.

$40,000 ÷ 570 hours = $70.18 per hour

Step 5. Decide if the rate seems reasonable. Does the rate seem reasonable? Consider what the market will bear. Your answer depends on the type of service you provide and your competition. If the rate is not reasonable, how can you adjust it? Is your salary goal too high? Can you reduce overhead expenses or increase billable hours? Can you accomplish this amount of work and manage your business while maintaining a reasonable schedule? Is this a viable business, given your financial and lifestyle goals?

Service Providers/Hourly Rate Worksheet

Annual Operating Expenses

Rent _____

Utilities + _____

Telephone + _____

Office supplies + _____

Postage + _____

Equipment repairs & maintenance + _____

Business insurance + _____

Loan payments + _____

Marketing costs + _____

Subscriptions/Dues/Fees + _____

Legal/Accounting + _____

(continued)

(continued)

Travel & entertainment + _____

Other _____ + _____

_____ _____

_____ _____

_____ _____

_____ _____

Total annual operating expenses: = _____

Owner's annual compensation: + _____

Self-employment taxes: + _____

Annual health insurance cost: + _____

#1. Total income required: = _____

Total working hours per year
(52 weeks x 40 hours) 2,080

Less vacation hours: – _____

Less holiday hours: – _____

#2. Available working hours per year = _____

Available working hours per quarter
(available hours per year ÷ 4) = _____

Estimated Billable Hours per Quarter

Available Hours per Quarter		Percent Billable Hours		Billable Hours per Quarter
Quarter 1: _____	x	_____	=	_____
Quarter 2: _____	x	_____	=	_____
Quarter 3: _____	x	_____	=	_____
Quarter 4: _____	x	_____	=	_____

#3. Estimated billable hours per year: = _____

#4. Total income ÷ **total billable** = **hourly rate:**
required **hours per year** = _____

#5. Is this reasonable? _____

Summing Up

After you have completed your analysis, ask yourself the following questions:

- **Does your pricing seem reasonable?** Consider what the market will bear. The answer depends on the products you are providing and your competition.

- **If your prices are not reasonable, can you adjust them?** Can you minimize your cost of goods sold without sacrificing quality? Can you reduce your fixed expenses? If so, how? Is your owner's compensation goal too high? Are there fixed expenses that can be eliminated? If your expenses cannot be reduced substantially, can your estimated sales be reasonably increased?

- **Taking into account your local competition, are your sales goals reasonable?** Also take into account your business hours. Are your sales estimates reasonable for the number of hours your business will be open?

- **If you will be providing the bulk of the labor, how many hours will it take for you to meet your production goals?** In the example of Mary's business, she may determine that she will have to work more hours for less personal income to be self-employed. If this is the case for you, ask yourself if that is consistent with your financial and lifestyle goals. Can you accomplish this amount of work and manage your business while maintaining a reasonable schedule?

The answers to these questions will help you decide if your business idea is a viable one.

Once you've made the commitment to start your business, track your actual expenses and sales. Compare your actual numbers to your original estimates. Review these numbers often and adjust your estimates accordingly. The longer your business operates, the more information you will have and the better your estimates will become.

CHAPTER 6

Finding, Reaching, and Serving Your Customers

Many people dream of starting a business so they can make a living doing work that they do well and love. But when you are just starting out, you'll find that you spend most of your time trying to find people who will pay you for your work. Although you are good at your chosen occupation, you may be uncomfortable when it comes to marketing your business. But marketing is one of the most important things you will do, not only as you start but also as you continue to run your businesses.

What does it mean to market your business? When you hear the word *marketing,* you may think of advertising, promotions, public relations, or market research. Indeed, marketing includes all of these. It sounds complicated and expensive. Some marketing departments in large corporations do have enormous budgets. But you can make your marketing efforts fun and inexpensive. Remember, you only get a chance to *sell* your product or service to your customers when they *know* about your product or service.

Marketing means making potential customers aware of your product or service and getting them to try it for the very first time.

Step-by-Step Marketing

Before you spend any money on advertising, take the time to research and consider the steps of marketing. When you are educated about your product or service and understand your customers, you are ready to make decisions about the best ways to reach your potential customers.

Step 1: Know your product

Step 2: Know your customers

Step 3: Know how to reach your customers

Step 4: Know your competition

Step 5: Know how to serve your customers

Step 1: Know Your Product

The first step in developing a marketing plan is to be very clear about what you are selling. You must be able to describe your product or service in clear, precise terms that anyone can understand. Before you can sell your product or service to a potential customer, you must be convinced that what you offer is terrific. Below are some questions to start you thinking about the best way to describe your product or service.

- What product or service do you provide? Don't forget to include support services you offer (for example, delivery, maintenance, and house calls).

  _____

  _____

- What makes your product or service special? How is your product or service different from ones that are already on the market?

  _____

  _____

- Why will people want to buy your product or service? _____

  _____

  _____

- Add any other information about your product or service you think is important.

  _____

  _____

One of the biggest mistakes beginning entrepreneurs make is not having a clear product or service to sell. They try to sell something to everyone. Their message gets lost and they confuse the consumer. As your business grows, you may be able to expand your services and products, but in the beginning, it's crucial to

- Focus!
- Focus!
- Focus!

Below are examples of entrepreneurs and their products and services. Read through the examples and decide who is ready to market to their potential customers, who is too narrowly focused, and who needs to focus their product or service.

A florist who does not provide a delivery service. _____

A small clothing store that offers punk styles, business outfits, maternity clothes, and formals. _____

A seamstress who sews new clothes and does alterations for middle-income women. She will make house calls or do fittings at her workshop by appointment. _____

A hairdresser who works alone, trying to develop a walk-in business and do home visits at the same time. _____

A caterer with excellent home-cooked food who puts care into arranging beautiful table displays. She does not provide servers, but has a list of people she can recommend.   ⎯⎯⎯⎯⎯

An upholsterer who does sewing and refinishing but expects customers to bring their own material.   ⎯⎯⎯⎯⎯

An experienced daycare provider who offers educational toys, snacks, a play area, and flexible hours.   ⎯⎯⎯⎯⎯

A delivery service that promises next-day delivery but does not pick up after noon.   ⎯⎯⎯⎯⎯

A single person doing roofing, indoor/outdoor painting, carpentry, and household repairs.   ⎯⎯⎯⎯⎯

A landscaper offering landscape design, a 15-percent discount arrangement with the local garden center, delivery, installation, and maintenance.   ⎯⎯⎯⎯⎯

A house painter emphasizing quality work but using a cheap grade of paint to save customers money.   ⎯⎯⎯⎯⎯

Step 2: Know Your Customers

The second step in developing a marketing plan is to determine who your potential customers are and what they are looking for. You have limited time and money, so it's important to target your resources to the people who are most likely to buy from you.

Who Are Your Customers?

When you think of your product or service, what common characteristics do you think your potential customers might have? If your customers will be organizations, what characteristics will they have in common?

Here are some characteristics to help you get started.

Individuals		Organizations
Income level	Job and position	Size
Sex, age, marital status	Religion	Profit/Not-for-profit
Education	Location	Number of employees
Health	Hobbies, skills	Location
Do-it-yourself types	Internal capabilities	
Race	Number of children	
Own or rent a home	Age and type of car	
Vacation activities	Household pets	
Eating habits	Buying habits	

Now that you've identified who your potential customers will be, take a look at what may be important to them.

What Are Your Customers Looking For?

Below is a list of qualities customers look for in products and services. Scan through them and then list in the space provided the three things you think are the most important to customers who would buy your product or service.

1. _____

2. _____

3. _____

- Durability
- Variety
- Ease of care
- Craftsmanship

- Style
- Promptness
- Efficiency

- Cost
- Reliability
- Comfort

Check Out the Market

There are several sources of information on the business community and customer base in your area. Check these out first; then brainstorm to come up with other possibilities.

- **The Internet:** Many sites can provide you with information about your potential market. A good place to begin your search is the U.S. Census Bureau site at http://www.census.gov.

- **The public library:** You can get information on the size and makeup of your market, the number of people per household, family income, the number of homeowners and home values, and the number of cars per household. This kind of information is available for both the national and local levels, so you can compare the two. Here are some of the information sources you will find at your local library:

  - *Encyclopedia of Associations* lists trade associations, including addresses and phone numbers and a list of publications.

  - *Measuring Markets: A Guide to the Use of Federal and State Statistical Data* will help you find specific publications with market information for the area that interests you.

  - *Census of Population and Housing, Standard Metropolitan Statistical Areas,* and *Census Tract Reports.*

  - *County Business Patterns* summarizes information on businesses by state and county. Information is provided by business type, number and size of businesses, and number of employees.

- **The Yellow Pages.**

- **Competitors:** Check out your competition's marketing literature, Web site, and publicity; observe their customers and how customers are treated; look at the same type of business in another community or town.

- Wholesalers and manufacturers.
- Federal and state governments.
- Business, trade, and professional journals and meetings.
- Chambers of commerce and local governments.
- Potential customers: Watch your potential customers in action or do interview surveys with them.

Step 3: Know How to Reach Your Customers

So now you've defined your product or service and you have an idea of who your customers will be. In this section, we look at several ways to make those potential customers aware of your product or service. Certain ideas will work better for some businesses than for others. However, every entrepreneur should remember one idea: Business is about relationships!

In most cases, it takes time for potential customers to become paying customers. In your personal life, you don't meet a person, spend a few minutes with him or her, and immediately become best friends. It's the same in business: It takes time for potential customers to understand and believe in the benefits of your product or service. As you spread the word about your product or service, you will meet lots of people who are interested in your business but who don't need or want to buy from you at that time. Consider and work with these people as potential customers.

Here are some simple ways to make your potential customers aware of your product or service and to encourage them to buy from you. Keep your profile of potential customers in mind as you consider these ideas.

Create a Professional Image

Earlier, we discussed the importance of a good name for your business. But there is more to creating an image than a name. Should you also consider a logo? What written materials will you need? Business cards? Stationery? Brochures? You can use software programs to create a professional image for all of your written materials. Consider Microsoft Publisher, FrontPage, or PhotoDraw. Other software programs to consider are Adobe Photoshop and CorelDraw.

Your business image comes across strongly on the phone. Think about how you will answer the phone and consider the image you want to give. If you have employees who answer the phones, you must take time to explain to them the image you are trying to create. You need to be sure that everything about your business reflects that *you are a professional.*

Many businesses today are located in private homes, and customers either don't know or don't care. However, if your business is located in your home and you are worried that it might make potential customers unsure if you can handle their business, you might consider renting a post office box or adding a suite number to your home address. You might also pay a little extra for a phone number that sounds businesslike (such as 595-1000).

What other equipment do you need to present a professional image? Remember, at the beginning of your business you need to concentrate on spending money on items that will bring you sales. You can always add equipment to your business as you have the funds available. So, depending on your business, you may want to consider a fax machine, cell phone, voice mail, e-mail address, or pager.

To get started thinking about your professional image, write your answer to this question in the space below: What do you want your image to say to your potential customers?

_____

_____

_____

_____

_____

_____

Network

Networking is a hot topic these days. We are acutely aware of the importance of networking to find a job, or even perhaps a mate, but you should use networking to market your business, too. That means being prepared to talk about your business to anyone and everyone. Your car mechanic may not be interested in buying your product or service, but his brother-in-law might become your best customer. Remember, business is about relationships.

> *Make sure you offer only what your market wants to buy.*

Always carry your business cards with you, and when you hand them out, give people two: one for themselves and one for someone they know who might be interested in your product or service. This list offers some more ideas to get you started networking:

- Become the expert in your field.
- Always do what you say you will do.
- Create a follow-up system so you will remember who and when to call.
- Stay in touch with previous customers.
- Always send thank-you notes.
- Follow up with a phone call after a week to be sure your customers are pleased with your product or service.
- Seize each and every opportunity.
- Consider "freebies" if they could mean sales in the future.
- Make networking calls every week.
- Join professional groups.
- Volunteer in local organizations.

Advertise

Most small businesses don't have the money to pay for an advertising blitz. The good news is that most small businesses don't need to advertise on a large scale. You will probably be better off if you appeal *directly to your target customers* by less-expensive means. If your business must advertise to larger markets, you should proceed carefully. Many microenterprises have lost vast amounts of money with no return by choosing the wrong advertising vehicles. You might attract more customers with a well-thought-out brochure mailed to people you *know* are potential customers than with an ad run once in a newspaper.

© *JIST Works*

Here are some basics you should keep in mind, however you choose to advertise:

- Make your message consistent.
- Create a learning experience for your customers.
- The secret to marketing is repetition.
- Try to create an element of surprise and fun.

This list contains some advertising methods you might consider. Some are more feasible than others for small businesses, but don't discount any of them without exploring all the possibilities.

- **Television** ads are short and fleeting, and it's difficult to be sure you're going to hit your target market. They also may be too expensive for your small business, but check with local cable stations before you completely rule them out. Cable stations are less expensive and may appeal to an audience that is close to your potential market. Local talk shows also may be perfect for your topic; many interview "experts" on a variety of topics. *You* may be the expert in your field.

- **Radio** is also expensive, but it's easier to get directly to your target market. Remember, however, that radio usually is background noise, so an ad on the radio takes many repetitions before people actually hear your message. Again, talk shows can be helpful in getting your message out.

- **Print advertising** includes ads in either magazines or newspapers. If you do some careful research, *you can get directly to your customers* with this medium. The impact of print, however, may build more slowly than other kinds of advertising. If your customers will contact you by phone to request your product or service, you might consider an ad in the Yellow Pages. Look at your competitors' ads. But keep this question in mind: How many customers each month will you need from that ad to make it cost-effective?

- **The press release** is a time-honored way of telling people you're in business, and you don't have to hire a professional to write one. Check your library for information on how a press release should look and what information it should include. Often local media are looking for good stories, so try to present your company as newsworthy. And don't forget to follow up with a phone call to answer questions about your press release. If appropriate, have your services listed in the calendar of events in your local newspaper or in any listing about changes in companies.

- **A Web site** for your business is often an easy and inexpensive way to provide exposure for your business. Your Internet service provider may offer a Web page free with your subscription. Explore software that provides you with a template to set up your Web page. Remember, if you have a Web site, you must let your customers know that you're on the Web. Be sure your Web address (URL) is included on all written materials–business cards, stationery, flyers, and so on—and submit it to Internet search engines such as Google (http://www.google.com) and Yahoo (http://www.yahoo.com).

- **Mail** is still one of the cheapest ways to get your information into the hands of your customers, but it also is one of the more difficult methods of advertising. If you are going to create a large direct-mail campaign and you don't want your hard work to get thrown out with the junk mail, you need to either thoroughly research your project or hire professional help. If you are mailing to your past customers and your own list of potential customers, always remember to maintain a professional image. Again, consult books in the library on setting up a direct-mail campaign.

- **Trade shows** are worth considering if you can find one geared to your product or services. Common estimates say that 86 percent of trade show attendees are there to buy. Your goal should be to meet as many people as possible so you can develop sales leads. Have a system to take names and addresses to add to your customer database, and be sure to follow up on all leads soon after the show.

- **Word of mouth** is probably the best advertising you can have, because your satisfied customers effectively become your sales force. It doesn't cost anything, but this method of marketing takes a while to develop.

Step 4: Know Your Competition

Who are your competitors? Is your competition trying to appeal to the same customers you are? Your answer to your competitors is simple: Create a niche. Your niche can be who you serve, what you do, where you do it, when you do it, or how you do it, or it can combine any of those factors. In the following space, list your competitors and identify their strengths and weaknesses. How do you compare with the competition on price, location, quality, service, and image?

My Direct Competitors

Competitor	Strengths	Weaknesses

Direct competition is another business that is selling a similar product or service to the same customers that your business is trying to reach. A small dress-making business catering to middle-class customers probably is not in competition with the local thrift shop or the designer floor of the downtown department store. But it might face serious competition from middle-range mail-order fashion catalogs.

If customers do not buy your product, where else can they find what they're looking for? Although another business may not be selling exactly the same product or service as yours, you may still consider it indirect competition if it is providing an alternative way for customers to meet their needs.

© *JIST Works*

For example, instead of hiring your phone-answering service, customers might buy answering machines; arrange with friends, family members, or colleagues to take messages; use call-forwarding; or make do without having calls answered. Choosing any one of these options prevents the customer from choosing your answering service. In the space below, jot down any indirect competition you need to consider.

Indirect competition I should consider:

_____

_____

_____

_____

Step 5: Know How to Serve Your Customers

American shoppers have become accustomed to horrible shopping experiences. Everyone has stories about a product that was defective, a sales associate who was rude, or being lost in a mammoth store with no help in sight. As the owner of a small business, you have much more control over the experiences of your customers. You can provide excellent customer service and exceed the customers' expectations with every transaction. Whenever you think about dealing with your customers, potential or actual, remember that good customer service can mean the difference between business success and failure. If you have trouble believing that, consider these facts:

- **Customers *will* tell a company where it needs improvement.** Ask your customers how you can make your business more suitable to them, *and then listen to what they say!*

- **Poor service is the #1 reason American companies lose business.** Most customers stop doing business with a company because of poor service.

- **The majority of customers who stop doing business with a company make no attempt to tell the firm why.**

- **Only a minority of dissatisfied customers ever complain.** Most dissatisfied customers don't complain because they believe it's not worth their time, the company won't listen, or the company won't do anything about the complaint.

- **The average dissatisfied customer tells many people about his or her dissatisfaction.**

- **It's commonly accepted that it takes $10 of new business to replace $1 of lost business.**

- **Quality of service is the main thing that differentiates one business from another.**

- **Customers are willing to pay more for better service.**

Summing Up

You may have the best product or service in your area, but if you have no customers, you will not be able to make money and maintain your business. The time to educate yourself about your product and your potential customers is *before* you begin your business. Ask lots of questions and *listen* to what people tell you. Remember, you are beginning to make business relationships, so it is important to always do what you tell people you will do.

CHAPTER 7

Managing Your Cash Flow

Successful business owners know how to manage the flow of cash coming into and going out of their businesses. They realize that even a profitable business can fail if no operating cash is available. Skillful cash-flow management results from proper planning. By making some simple forecasts, you can learn to project your cash-flow requirements. Experience will improve your ability to create sound cash-flow projections.

In this chapter, you learn to create useful projections to help you manage your cash flow.

What Is Cash Flow?

Cash flow, as the name implies, is simply the flow of cash coming into and going out of your business. You achieve positive cash flow when money comes into your business faster than it goes out. Because a business must have cash to operate, you must maintain positive cash flow in order to survive. Positive cash flow is a matter of timing. Managing your cash flow is a matter of planning.

Having cash is not the same as being profitable. It is possible for a business to have cash and be operating at a loss. For example, if you start your business with $10,000 in the bank and you operate at a loss of $1,000 each month, how many months can you stay in business and have cash in the bank? It also is possible for a business to be making a profit and have no cash. For example, if you are operating at a profit and extending 60-day credit terms to your customers but paying your suppliers upon delivery, how long will you be able to keep operating before you run out of cash?

This concept is important to understand, because many small business owners believe that as long as they have cash in the bank, they must be making a profit. That can be a dangerous assumption.

Small business owners tend to neglect the task of business management. There are many important things a business owner must do: make sales, produce products, provide services, compete for customers. Owners often spend so much time "being" the business that they don't take time to "manage" the business. This is a common mistake that results in the business "managing" the owner.

> *Manage your business, or your business will manage you.*

As a business owner, you will probably face cash-flow management tasks daily. If you don't start with a plan, you'll spend a great deal of time reacting to instead of anticipating events. You may find yourself trying to placate suppliers, struggling to make loan payments, hoping for a miracle so you can make payroll, and losing sleep over how to keep your utilities from being disconnected (again). The result is that you have even less time to make sales, produce products, provide services, and compete for customers—plus you will have strained important relationships with your creditors. In the long run, you create more stress for yourself if you don't manage your business. Avoid the trap of being managed by your business: Learn to manage your cash flow.

Projecting Cash Flow

Take a look at an example of a business where no cash-flow management has taken place. Like so many business owners, Cathy Smith, the owner of Cathy's Cleaning Service, believes she has no time to project and manage her cash flow.

Cathy's Cleaning Service

Cathy Smith owns a residential and commercial cleaning business. She has four part-time employees (one of whom is her mother) who work in two cleaning crews. Each crew works the same monthly schedule, cleaning two commercial buildings and seven homes.

Cathy also cleans newly constructed homes for a local builder and vacated apartments for a property management company. She cleans these herself.

Her residential customers pay for cleaning services as they are performed by leaving checks for the crews to deliver to Cathy at the end of each day. The two commercial buildings are invoiced once a month with 30-day terms. Cathy invoices the construction company and property manager as she cleans for them, and they usually pay her within 15 days.

Cathy reimburses her employees for mileage expenses to travel to job sites. She includes these reimbursements with the paychecks each Friday afternoon.

Cathy has no cash-flow plan; she is much too busy cleaning to create one each month.

Let's look at Cathy's cash flow for the month of August.

Cathy's Cleaning Service, Before...

Week 1	Ending Bank Balance
Cathy starts the week with $75.	$ 75.00
1. She collects $180 from residential homes.	$255.00
2. Cathy gets a check for $280 for new homes cleaned two weeks ago.	$535.00
3. Payroll this week is $435.	$100.00
4. Mileage reimbursements total $25.	$ 75.00
5. Cathy needs $12.50 to reimburse herself for mileage.	$ 62.50
Cathy ends week one with $62.50.	$ 62.50

© JIST Works

Week 2

6. Residential homes pay $225 this week. $287.50

7. A new home Cathy cleaned two weeks ago pays $70. $357.50

8. Payroll is $435, which leaves Cathy short. She asks her mother not to
    cash her check, but her mother cannot afford to do this.   ($77.50)

9. Employee mileage reimbursements are $27. Cathy isn't sure what to do.   ($104.50)

Cathy ends the week with a negative bank balance and worries that the
checks will hit the bank before she can cover them.   ($104.50)

Week 3

10. Cathy hears from the bank immediately: Her account is charged a
    $25 NSF fee.   ($129.50)

11. Cathy borrows $150 from a friend, who is not happy about it. $ 20.50

12. Residential homes pay $180. $200.50

13. Building No. 2 pays $350 for one month. $550.50

14. Payroll this week is $435. Employees murmur and rush to the bank. $115.50

15. Employee mileage reimbursements are $26. $ 89.50

16. Cathy must spend $50 on cleaning supplies. $ 39.50

17. Cathy needs $12.50 for gas for her car. $ 27.00

18. An apartment she cleaned last month pays her $82. $109.00

Cathy ends this week with $109, an angry friend, upset employees,
and a serious headache. $109.00

Week 4

19. Cathy collects $225 from residential customers. $334.00

20. Building No. 1 pays a $500 monthly cleaning bill. $834.00

21. Payroll is $435, and Cathy is thrilled she has the cash. $399.00

22. Cathy's angry friend insists on repayment of the $150 loan now! $249.00

23. Employee mileage reimbursements total $26. $223.00

24. A new home Cathy cleaned two weeks ago pays $100. $323.00

25. Cathy needs gas for her car again: $12.50. $310.50

26. Cathy finally pays herself a salary for the month: $200. $110.50

Cathy ends the month with $110.50 and the dread of facing another
month of similar struggles! $110.50

Cathy Makes a Plan

1. Cathy knows how much and when she will collect from residential customers.

2. Cathy's payroll amount remains about the same each week.

3. Her commercial accounts are on contract and pay the same amount each month.

4. Cathy knows how much she will have to reimburse her employees for mileage.

5. Cathy can make an educated guess about how much income she will collect from cleaning new houses and vacant apartments. She also can ask the new homes builder and the apartment manager to give her an estimate at the beginning of each month, since they know when they will need her weeks before they call her.

Given all that Cathy knows and can assume, she can draw a "picture" of when cash is going to come in and when it is going out. It would look like the table below.

Cathy's Cleaning Service

Date	Description	Cash In	Cash Out	Balance
				$ 75.00
Week 1	Homes	$180.00		$255.00
	New Homes	$280.00		$535.00
	Payroll		$435.00	$100.00
	Mileage		$ 25.00	$ 75.00
	Gasoline		$ 12.50	$ 62.50
Week 2	Homes	$225.00		$287.50
	New Home	$ 70.00		$357.50
	Payroll		$435.00	($ 77.50)
	Mileage		$ 27.00	($104.50)
Week 3	NSF		$ 25.00	($129.50)
	Loan	$150.00		$ 20.50
	Homes	$180.00		$200.50
	Building #2	$350.00		$550.50
	Payroll		$435.00	$115.50
	Mileage		$ 26.00	$ 89.50
	Cleaning Sup		$ 50.00	$ 39.50
	Gasoline		$ 12.50	$ 27.00
	Apartment	$ 82.00		$109.00
Week 4	Homes	$225.00		$334.00
	Building #1	$500.00		$834.00
	Payroll		$435.00	$399.00
	Repay Loan		$150.00	$249.00
	Mileage		$ 26.00	$223.00
	New Home	$100.00		$323.00
	Gasoline		$ 12.50	$310.50
	Cathy		$200.00	$110.50
		$2,342.00	$2,306.50	$110.50

© JIST Works

Without any plan, Cathy didn't know she was going to run out of cash. After she created her plan, she was able to come up with some short-term solutions for her anticipated cash shortages. More importantly, Cathy has seen the need to come up with some long-term solutions to avoid future shortages.

Here are some other ideas that might help Cathy improve her cash-flow plan.

1. Cathy invoices her commercial customers only once a month, even though she cleans for them every week. They pay her invoices according to her terms: within 30 days. Cathy could start sending invoices on a weekly basis. The invoice amounts would be smaller (one week of cleaning instead of one month), but the payments would come in faster.

2. Cathy pays her employees and reimburses their mileage expenses once a week. She could change her payroll and mileage reimbursements to once every two weeks (26 times per year) or, better yet, twice a month (24 times per year). This would allow Cathy to hold on to her cash longer.

3. Instead of paying for her supplies in cash, Cathy could establish credit accounts with her primary suppliers. Again, Cathy would hold on to her cash longer.

> *Positive cash flow is a matter of timing.*

In the tables that follow, you can see the effects of these three simple changes on Cathy's cash flow.

Notice that Cathy didn't collect any more cash from her commercial accounts, she just collected it faster. She did not pay her employees any less, she just held on to her cash longer. Cathy still was able to buy cleaning supplies when she needed them, she just deferred payment.

As a result of these changes, Cathy didn't bounce any payroll checks, which made her employees happy. She didn't need to borrow money from her friend, which made her friend happy. She avoided the bank's NSF charges, which made her bank happy. And she was left with considerably higher cash balances at the end of each week, which made Cathy very happy. She also begins the new month with a higher cash balance and a management plan.

Predicting the (Cash) Future

It doesn't take a crystal ball to project your cash future. What it does take is some educated guessing. The longer you are in business and the more experience you acquire, the better your guesses will be.

Cathy's Cleaning Service, Before...

Date	Description	Deposits	Checks	Balance
				$ 75.00
Week 1	Homes	$180.00		$255.00
	New Homes	$280.00		$535.00
	Payroll		$435.00	$100.00
	Mileage		$ 25.00	$ 75.00
	Gasoline		$ 12.50	$ 62.50
Week 2	Homes	$225.00		$287.50
	New Home	$ 70.00		$357.50
	Payroll		$435.00	($ 77.50)
	Mileage		$ 27.00	($104.50)
Week 3	NSF		$ 25.00	($129.50)
	Loan	$150.00		$ 20.50
	Homes	$180.00		$200.50
	Building #2	$350.00		$550.50
	Payroll		$435.00	$115.50
	Mileage		$ 26.00	$ 89.50
	Cleaning Sup		$ 50.00	$ 39.50
	Gasoline		$ 12.50	$ 27.00
	Apartment	$ 82.00		$109.00
Week 4	Homes	$225.00		$334.00
	Building #1	$500.00		$834.00
	Payroll		$435.00	$399.00
	Repay Loan		$150.00	$249.00
	Mileage		$ 26.00	$223.00
	New Home	$100.00		$323.00
	Gasoline		$ 12.50	$310.50
	Cathy		$200.00	$110.50
		$2,342.00	$2,306.50	$110.50

© JIST Works

Cathy's Cleaning Service, After...

Date	Description	Deposits	Checks	Balance
				$ 75.00
Week 1	Homes	$180.00		$255.00
	New Homes	$280.00		$535.00
	Building #1	$125.00		$660.00
	Building #2	$ 87.50		$747.50
	Gasoline		$ 12.50	$735.00
Week 2	Homes	$225.00		$960.00
	New Home	$ 70.00		$1,030.00
	Building #1	$125.00		$1,155.00
	Building #2	$ 87.50		$1,242.50
	Payroll/2 wks		$870.00	$372.50
	Mileage/2 wks		$ 52.00	$320.50
Week 3	Homes	$180.00		$500.50
	Building #1	$125.00		$625.50
	Building #2	$ 87.50		$713.00
	Apartment	$ 82.00		$795.00
	Gasoline		$ 12.50	$782.50
Week 4	Homes	$225.00		$1,007.50
	Building #1	$125.00		$1,132.50
	Building #2	$ 87.50		$1,220.00
	Payroll/2 wks		$870.00	$350.00
	Mileage/2 wks		$ 52.00	$298.00
	New Home	$100.00		$398.00
	Gasoline		$ 12.50	$385.50
	Cathy		$200.00	$185.50
		$2,192.00	$2,081.50	$185.50

Cathy saved herself the $25.00 NSF fee, plus she owes a supplier $50.00 for cleaning supplies, which is payable in 30 days.

To create cash-flow projections, take the information you know plus information you assume and apply it to a calendar or a time line. Not all businesses are as predictable as Cathy's Cleaning Service. Some information may be easy to predict: For example, your rent is a fixed amount that is due on the first day of each month; your telephone bill is usually $150, due on the 25th; and your insurance premiums are payable once a quarter. Other information is more difficult to forecast: How much will sale revenues be in January? Will this be a harsh winter with extraordinarily high heating bills? Will you suffer costly equipment failures?

When preparing your cash-flow projections, there are other things to consider, as well. Will seasonal fluctuations, holidays, or events in your community have an impact on your business? Will a convention in town mean more or less business for you? What about sporting events? How about plans for road construction? Will the weather affect your business? What about annual conventions for your industry?

Whether you are establishing a new business or managing an existing one, think of ways to stretch your dollars to improve your cash flow. This might mean renegotiating credit terms with customers or suppliers. If this is the case, schedule time to do it. Remember, time spent managing your business ensures that your business does not manage you! Be creative! List ways you can create a positive cash flow for your business:

_____

_____

_____

_____

_____

_____

_____

_____

_____

_____

_____

_____

Tip: There are computer programs available that can make preparing cash-flow projections easier, including electronic spreadsheets and simple-to-use accounting software (such as the Quicken and QuickBooks products by Intuit, Inc.). Whether you do projections manually or on a computer, you need to gather and calculate the same information.

© JIST Works

Sandra's Sewing Circle

In this exercise, account for start-up cash flow in and start-up cash flow out; then estimate four consecutive weeks of operation in a new business. Complete the worksheet using these assumptions:

1. Sandra's Sewing Circle begins with a cash balance of $0.00. She will make an owner's investment of $1,000 and add a no-interest loan from her mother of $500.

2. Sandra will have to pay an $80 deposit to the phone company for service, as well as a $50 business license fee to the city.

3. Sandra will purchase $450 of start-up inventory. She already owns most of her own equipment, and she is setting up her business in a friend's shop.

4. Sandra is now ready to start estimating her operating expenses. In the first week, Sandra will begin paying her friend $40 a week for rent. Sandra thinks she will do $120 of business, for which she will be paid in cash. Sandra will have to pay $75 for a previous delivery of business cards and stationery. She estimates an additional purchase of fabrics for $40.

5. In her second week of business, Sandra estimates income of $145. She estimates that her share of the electric bill will be $20. She knows she will have an insurance premium of $75. Sandra wants to draw $150 for her own salary. Additional fabrics should be around $50.

6. In week 3, Sandra hopes to bring in $200 of sales income from a high school band account, as well as $45 of retail business. She will pay for her ad in the neighborhood newspaper, which will cost $25. She estimates a purchase of fabrics at a cost of $75.

7. Sandra estimates income of only $120 in week 4. Sandra will have to pay her mother $200 against her loan this week. She also wants to pay herself another $150. Sandra estimates her telephone bill at $60 and additional fabrics at $40.

On the following pages are two start-up cash-flow worksheets and two cash-flow worksheets for an existing business. Complete the first start-up worksheet using the information about Sandra's Sewing Circle. Use the other worksheets to make cash-flow projections for your own business.

Start-Up Business Cash-Flow Worksheet

	Start-up cash flow	Week 1	Week 2	Week 3	Week 4
1. Beginning cash					
Cash in					
2. Owner's investment					
3. Loan proceeds					
4. Sales income					
5. Other:					
6. Total cash in (add lines 2-5)					
Cash out/start-up					
7. Initial rent/deposits					
8. Initial utility/deposits					
9. Equipment purchases/deposits					
10. Initial inventory purchases					
11. Initial office supply purchases					
12. Fees/License					
13. Other:					
14. Other:					
Cash out					
15. COGS, labor					
16. COGS, materials					
17. Rent					
18. Insurance					
19. Payroll					
20. Payroll taxes					
21. Loan payments					
22. Advertising/Marketing					
23. Travel expenses					
24. Owner's compensation					
25. Office supplies					
26. Telephone					
27. Utilities					
28. Other:					

© JIST Works

	Start-up cash flow	Week 1	Week 2	Week 3	Week 4
29. Other:					
30. Other:					
31. Other:					
32. Other:					
33. Total cash out (add lines 7-32)					
34. Change in cash (line 6 minus line 33)					
35. Ending cash (line 1 plus line 34)					

Note: Ending cash for one period becomes the beginning cash for the next period.

Start-Up Business Cash-Flow Worksheet

	Start-up cash flow	Week 1	Week 2	Week 3	Week 4
1. Beginning cash					
Cash in					
2. Owner's investment					
3. Loan proceeds					
4. Sales income					
5. Other:					
6. Total cash in (add lines 2-5)					
Cash out/start-up					
7. Initial rent/deposits					
8. Initial utility/deposits					
9. Equipment purchases/deposits					
10. Initial inventory purchases					
11. Initial office supply purchases					
12. Fees/License					
13. Other:					
14. Other:					

(continued)

(continued)

	Start-up cash flow	Week 1	Week 2	Week 3	Week 4
Cash out					
15. COGS, labor					
16. COGS, materials					
17. Rent					
18. Insurance					
19. Payroll					
20. Payroll taxes					
21. Loan payments					
22. Advertising/Marketing					
23. Travel expenses					
24. Owner's compensation					
25. Office supplies					
26. Telephone					
27. Utilities					
28. Other:					
29. Other:					
30. Other:					
31. Other:					
32. Other:					
33. Total cash out (add lines 7-32)					
34. Change in cash (line 6 minus line 33)					
35. Ending cash (line 1 plus line 34)					

Note: Ending cash for one period becomes the beginning cash for the next period.

© JIST Works

Existing Business Cash-Flow Worksheet

	Period 1		Period 2		Period 3	
	Projected	Actual	Projected	Actual	Projected	Actual
1. Beginning cash						
Cash in						
2. Owner's investment						
3. Loan proceeds						
4. Sales income						
5. Other:						
6. Total cash in (add lines 2-5)						
Cash out						
7. COGS, labor						
8. COGS, materials						
9. Rent						
10. Insurance						
11. Payroll						
12. Payroll taxes						
13. Loan payments						
14. Advertising/Marketing						
15. Travel expenses						
16. Owner's compensation						
17. Office supplies						
18. Telephone						
19. Utilities						
20. Other:						
21. Other:						
22. Other:						
23. Other:						
24. Other:						
25. Total cash out (add lines 7-24)						
26. Change in cash (line 6 minus line 25)						
27. Ending cash (line 1 plus line 26)						

Note: Ending cash for one period becomes the beginning cash for the next period.

Existing Business Cash-Flow Worksheet

	Period 1		Period 2		Period 3	
	Projected	**Actual**	**Projected**	**Actual**	**Projected**	**Actual**
1. Beginning cash						
Cash in						
2. Owner's investment						
3. Loan proceeds						
4. Sales income						
5. Other:						
6. Total cash in (add lines 2-5)						
Cash out						
7. COGS, labor						
8. COGS, materials						
9. Rent						
10. Insurance						
11. Payroll						
12. Payroll taxes						
13. Loan payments						
14. Advertising/Marketing						
15. Travel expenses						
16. Owner's compensation						
17. Office supplies						
18. Telephone						
19. Utilities						
20. Other:						
21. Other:						
22. Other:						
23. Other:						
24. Other:						
25. Total cash out (add lines 7-24)						
26. Change in cash (line 6 minus line 25)						
27. Ending cash (line 1 plus line 26)						

Note: Ending cash for one period becomes the beginning cash for the next period.

© JIST Works

What Does Your Lender Want?

If you intend to approach a lender for funds, a *cash-flow projection,* or financial plan (see Chapter 3), will be one of the most important documents you submit. You should make your cash-flow projection for at least one year, maybe longer, depending on the requirements of the lender.

It is common for a start-up business to show negative cash balances in the first year. Most lenders expect your projections to show a cash break-even point around the end of the first year and show positive cash flow in subsequent years. You must be prepared to show the lender how you plan to handle negative cash flow. Are you seeking a loan or a line of credit to cover the entire negative cash balance? Do you also have personal resources you will be contributing? Do you have investors with available cash?

Because projections are only estimates of what will happen, it's a good idea to submit at least three projections for the same period: a worst-case scenario, a likely scenario, and a best-case scenario. Be as realistic as possible in your projections. (Many lenders will still discount your projections as too optimistic.)

If you are seeking a loan, your projections must include a "cash in" line to show the loan proceeds coming into the business. Identify how those proceeds will be spent under "cash out." Will there be equipment or inventory purchases? Don't forget to include another "cash out" line reflecting your scheduled loan payments. Your lender will look for indications that you will use the loan proceeds to generate income. He or she also will evaluate how wisely you are using cash. Obviously, your projections must demonstrate an ability to pay back the loan out of cash flow. Ask your accountant or business advisor to review your projections before you submit them.

Summing Up

Cash-flow management can be a challenge in a small business. The key to effective cash-flow management is proper planning, which allows you to anticipate events—not just react to them. Remember: Manage your business, or your business will manage you!

The Business of Business

How do you make your business legal? Should you incorporate? Are you a limited partnership? In this chapter, we look at choosing the legal form of business that suits you best. It's important to choose one that will save you taxes and accommodate your family considerations. We also look at the special insurance needs of a new business, examine different types of insurance, discuss how to create a plan that meets your needs, and consider some important criteria for choosing an insurance agent.

Legal Forms of Business

You can choose from several types of business entities for your business. The most common are sole proprietorships, partnerships, and corporations. In this section, we examine each of these in more detail.

Sole Proprietorships

The simplest form of business is a *sole proprietorship,* which merely indicates that the business is owned and run by an individual acting alone. The owner has total control. If the owner dies or is incapacitated, the business ceases to function. The owner is solely responsible for debts and obligations of the business. Take a look at some of the advantages and disadvantages of this kind of business arrangement.

Advantages
- It requires the least amount of red tape to create and run.
- It is the least expensive to set up.
- You are your own boss.

Disadvantages
- You are completely responsible for all aspects of the business.
- Getting outside investments is difficult.
- Any debts or claims brought against the business are your personal responsibility.

Tax Ramifications
- Any profit or loss is declared on your personal income tax form.
- Profits generated by the business are taxable income to the owner.

- Profits are subject to payment of Social Security (FICA) taxes.
- The sole proprietor's salary is not tax-deductible because he or she is not considered an employee.

Forming a Sole Proprietorship

- It's very simple to form a sole proprietorship. Get a booklet from your local Secretary of State's office.

General Partnerships

A *partnership* is an association of two or more persons to carry on as co-owners of a business for profit. There are two kinds of partnerships. *General partners* are the people who run or manage a business. They have *unlimited liability*. *Limited partners* are investors who own a share of the business but don't run or manage it on a day-to-day basis. *Their liability is limited to the amount they have invested in the business.* The dissolution of a partnership may be caused by events such as the expulsion, death, bankruptcy, or withdrawal of a partner.

Advantages

- Partners are motivated to apply their best abilities by direct sharing of the profits.
- You are not alone.

Disadvantages

- At least one partner bears unlimited liability for the business.
- It is relatively difficult to obtain large sums of capital.
- The firm is bound by the acts of just one partner as agent.

Tax Ramifications

- Profits or losses are divided between the partners and are declared on their personal income tax returns.
- As partnerships do not pay taxes, they are merely required to file information returns.
- Taxation of the profit earned by the general partnership is passed through to the individual partners in proportion to each partner's distributive share of the general partnership's profit.
- Such income is subject to the payment of FICA taxes.
- Partnerships must withhold and remit FICA and unemployment insurance (FUTA) taxes.

Forming a General Partnership

- Forming a general partnership is a simple process. Check with your local Secretary of State's office for instructions.

© *JIST Works*

Limited Liability Company (LLC)

A *Limited Liability Company*, commonly called an LLC, is a business structure that combines the best features of partnerships and corporations. The LLC functions like a partnership because it is not a separate taxable entity. Like a partnership, the profits or losses of the LLC are reported on the partners' personal income tax reports. However, like a corporation, the LLC offers the protection from personal liability for business debts. *Limited liability* means that if the business owes money or is involved in a lawsuit, only the assets of the business itself are at risk—not the owners' personal assets.

Advantages

- Profits or losses are divided between the owners and are declared on their personal income tax returns.
- The LLC, not the individuals involved, is liable for any debt.
- Unlike corporations, the LLC has no restrictions on the number of shareholders who must be U.S. residents.
- In most states, one person can be the sole owner of a LLC.
- It is relatively easy to convert a sole proprietorship or partnership to a LLC. Some states provide a form called a certificate of conversion.

Disadvantages

- Not all businesses can operate as an LLC. Businesses in the banking, trust, and insurance industries are typically prohibited from forming an LLC. Some states, including California, prohibit professionals such as architects, accountants, doctors, and other licensed health-care workers from forming an LLC.
- If a written operating agreement is not part of the articles of organization, the LLC will be governed by the default rules in the filing state.

Tax Ramifications

- The LLC does not generally pay any income taxes itself. Instead, each LLC owner pays taxes on their share of profits or deducts their share of losses on their personal tax return.
- LLC owners can elect to have their LLC taxed like a corporation. This would reduce taxes for owners who need to retain a significant amount of profits in the company.

Forming a Limited Liability Company

- In most states, the Secretary of State's office handles the formation of LLCs. Many states require you to file an article of organization; some states call it a certificate of organization. Although most states do not require a written operating agreement, you should include it with your filing. The operating agreement helps to ensure that the courts will respect your personal liability protection. The agreement also lays out the rules that govern how profits will be split and how major business decisions will be made.

Corporations

By law, a corporation must meet all four of the following criteria: It has (1) limited liability, (2) free transferability of interests, (3) centralized management, and (4) continuity of life. A corporation is managed by a board of directors, which is elected by shareholders. The board of directors, in turn, elects officers to run the day-to-day operations of the business. Unlike other forms of business entities, a corporation continues to exist indefinitely unless it is merged with another corporation or dissolved. Interests in corporations are freely transferable, and shareholders are not personally liable for the debts and obligations of the corporation, unless the articles of incorporation provide otherwise.

In order to maintain the limited liability of shareholders, a corporation must observe the corporate formalities of keeping records, holding meetings of the shareholders and the board of directors, paying appropriate taxes, and filing required documents with the local Secretary of State, including annual reports. The failure to properly organize a corporation can subject the shareholders to personal liability. If a corporation fails to operate as a corporation, its creditors may attempt to "pierce the corporate veil" and assert claims against the shareholders personally.

Advantages

- Corporations have a much easier time, in general, getting investors.
- Corporations have a legal existence separate from the owners or investors.
- If one or more of the officers or investors leaves, the business can still go on.
- The corporation, not the individuals involved, is liable for any losses.
- Each person can lose only what he or she has invested.
- Liability is limited (but see the Disadvantages section).

Disadvantages

- New corporations often cannot get credit without the owners making personal guarantees.

Tax Ramifications

- For a regular corporation, the taxes are paid directly by the corporation. For a Subchapter S corporation, the profits or losses are divided among the investors. Investors receive their shares of the profits or losses and declare them on their personal income taxes.

C Corporation

- The corporate entity pays taxes on its taxable income.
- If and when distributions are made to shareholders, such income is taxed at the shareholder level as well. Taxation at both the corporate and shareholder levels is known as *double taxation.*

© *JIST Works*

S Corporation

- The corporation is not taxed on its income, but the individual shareholders are taxed on their shares of the corporation's profits, which are passed through to them.
- In order to qualify as an S corporation, the corporation can have no more than 35 shareholders. Only individuals, certain estates, and qualified trusts can be shareholders, and there can be no more than one class of stock.
- An S corporation also may not be a member of an affiliated group, which means that an S corporation may not own another corporation.
- An S corporation is generally not subject to state gross income tax, adjusted gross income tax, or supplemental net income tax.

Forming a Corporation

- Forming a corporation is more complicated than the other business forms, but it is not too difficult. You can file the necessary paperwork yourself. Pick up a booklet at your local Secretary of State's office.

What legal form will work best for your new business? In the space below, write down your answer; then list your reasons for making the choice.

_____

_____

_____

_____

It is important to choose a legal form that will work for you and your business. Talk to an accountant, who can review your personal financial situation and your vision for your business, before you make a final decision.

Choose the Best Business Form

Now read through the following scenarios and decide which would be the best business form for each: sole proprietorship, partnership, S corporation, or C corporation.

Susan's Secretarial Service

Susan has been a legal secretary working for the same attorney for the last 10 years. He is retiring at the end of the year, so Susan must make a career move. For years she has dreamed of owning her own business, and she thinks this might be a good time to pursue that dream. She knows several people in the legal community, and she knows that most law firms have an overabundance of work. She thinks she can contract with several firms for some of their overload. She wants to work from her home and already has all of the necessary equipment to get started. What would be the best business form for her?

_____

Movin' on Down the Road

Nicholas graduated from college six months ago and has been looking for a job ever since. He's been forced to move back home, and his parents are beginning to lose patience with him. His friend Michael spent the last five summers working for a large moving company and now has big plans to open his own moving company. His idea is to concentrate on local moves for individuals and office moves for companies. Michael has done his homework, is sure of his market, and has convinced Nicholas to go into the business with him on a 50-50 basis. What would be the best business form for them?

Hogin, Johnson, & Associates

Darlene Hogin and Cynthia Johnson are good friends who work for a community development corporation (CDC). Darlene's main responsibility is writing proposals to government agencies and private foundations requesting funding for CDC programs and operations. Cynthia is the vice-president of operations. Darlene and Cynthia are unhappy working for their organization and decide to strike out on their own as consultants to other CDCs. With their combined skills, they're sure they will be successful. What would be the best business form for them?

Pamper Your Pet

Kathy and Mark Smith are devoted pet lovers. They both have high-paying jobs, but neither is very happy with his or her career path. They've talked about starting a family, but they can't imagine how they will care for a child since they both work such long hours.

Last Sunday, Kathy saw an ad in the paper for a pet grooming business that is for sale. She called the following morning. The owner said he would be willing to stay on until Kathy is completely trained. The price sounds fair. If Mark keeps his job and Kathy starts the new business, they can make it financially and maybe start that family. They agree to move ahead with the idea. What would be the best business form for them?

Designs by Debbie

Debbie has always considered herself an artist. She has a good computer with several graphic design programs, and she continually upgrades her equipment. She loves designing and creating all kinds of paper products. Several friends have asked her to make invitations to parties. She has even produced several wedding invitations. Sometimes her friends offer to pay her, but she doesn't feel right taking money for something she loves doing.

Recently, her friends have encouraged her to test the market to see if there is a niche for her design business. She is reluctant, but she is tempted by the idea of making money in her own business doing the work she loves so much. If she decides to start a business, what would be the best business form for her?

© JIST Works

Ben's Best Brew

Ben has a beer recipe he is convinced would be a best seller. He has tested it out on many friends, and all agree that it has a great and unusual taste. Ben has done a lot of research, and he's found that it would take about $200,000 to start producing and marketing his product. He has a well-written and well-thought-out business plan, and he has approached several banks, but he hasn't been able to generate any interest.

So Ben decides to approach some of his friends to see if they might be interested in buying stock in his company. He invites several friends to a Sunday brunch at his house (serving his own beer, of course) to explain the plan and ask if any of them might be interested. Although only two people say yes, Ben is convinced he'll be able to come up with enough capital to start. If he decides to start a business, what would be the best business form for him?

Insuring Your Success

As you start your business, you must consider areas for which you need insurance coverage. You don't want to insure things unnecessarily, but you also don't want to take unreasonable chances with your business.

Types of Insurance

- **Homeowner's or renter's insurance** protects your home and furnishings and often includes several types of protection, including fire, theft, and damage. If you plan to run your business from your home, be sure to find out if the coverage applies when your residence is used for business purposes.
- **Fire insurance** protects solely against fire. This may be covered by your homeowner's policy. Again, you should check to see if having a business in your home changes the coverage in any way.
- **Liability insurance** protects you against claims from people who are injured as a result of dealing with you or your business.
- **Automobile insurance** obviously covers your car. Make sure to buy liability insurance that covers injury to employees or other parties. Your current policy probably will be affected by business use.
- **Workers' compensation insurance** is something you must have if you have employees. It protects you and your employees in case someone is injured on the job.
- **Business interruption insurance** protects you if your business is forced to close unexpectedly—because of a fire or a natural disaster, for example.
- **Key person insurance** protects you from the loss of key personnel.
- **Crime insurance** protects you from outside crime, such as vandalism, break-ins, or robberies.
- **A blanket dishonesty bond** protects you from loss from dishonest employees.
- **Glass insurance** protects you from the expense of replacing broken windows.

- **Computer insurance** covers the cost of replacing your computer in case of fire, theft, or accidents. (You should always have a backup of your data!)

- **Rent insurance** guarantees payment of your rent, even if your business income is interrupted by damage from weather or fire.

- **Employee benefits coverage** is unusual for a micro-business to provide. Usually a business must employ several people before this kind of insurance is affordable. Examples of employee benefit insurance policies include group life, group health, dental, and disability.

You should be aware of other alternatives to purchasing insurance. Some of the alternatives may be acceptable for your business.

- **Noninsurance** is ignoring the risk. This is used for all speculative risks. It is not the same as self-insurance.

- **Loss prevention programs** include wellness programs, safety procedures, training, and equipment such as burglar alarms and smoke detectors.

- **Transfer of risk** is exemplified by leasing vehicles from a company that would carry the insurance, hiring employees through temporary agencies, or drop shipping rather than storing inventory.

- **Self-insurance** is when you put money aside to cover possible losses.

Steps for Insurance Planning

1. **Evaluate the risks.** Think through where your business is at risk. What losses could your business not afford to cover without insurance?

2. **Set your priorities.** There will be some kinds of insurance you cannot afford to buy and others you can't afford *not* to buy. First, buy insurance for whatever could cause you the greatest loss. Remember, if you are the sole owner or a partner, anything you own personally can be taken to cover your business debts. The chance of a loss might be small, but it might also be a chance you can't afford to take. Decide which kinds of insurance you must have. List other kinds of insurance you would like to have. Decide which is most important.

3. **Make a plan.** Write down what insurance you need and what you want it to do for you.

4. **Find an agent.** Make sure the agent is someone you can trust. If possible, ask friends for agents they trust.

5. **Be economical.** Work with your agent to find the policy that is best for you. There are a number of ways you can get more insurance for your money, including these:

   ○ Compare prices between companies. (Be sure you are comparing prices for the same coverage.)

   ○ Carry as high a deductible as you can afford.

   ○ Avoid buying insurance for something already covered in another policy. Buy package plans if they fit what you need.

   ○ Buy very specific policies if you don't need more general coverage. (For example, don't pay big bucks for a renter's policy if all you want to cover is your computer.)

© *JIST Works*

6. **Keep good records.** Keep complete records of all policies, including type of coverage, name of insurer, dates the coverage is effective, annual premiums, claims for losses, and amounts received. Make sure to review your coverage at least once a year. And any time there are changes that might affect your coverage, let your agent know immediately.

7. **Get expert advice.** Consult an insurance specialist who isn't trying to sell you a policy. *Be sure you have a solid plan, because you have everything to lose if you don't.* This is an area of business for which everyone should seek expert advice.

Choose the Right Insurance

Now read the following case studies and decide which type(s) of insurance each of these businesses *must have* and what other type(s) of insurance they should consider.

Sam's Sod Design

Sam runs a landscaping business. He has a truck and several pieces of motorized equipment. He is the sole owner of the business, but he often employs people to help with jobs. Almost all of the work is done at job sites, but he does rent a garage to store his equipment.

Kendra's Christmas Cuties

Kendra makes hand-decorated Christmas stockings. She and a friend work out of her house. She has a couple of sewing machines and an embroidering machine. Kendra builds up stock from January through August, which she stores in her attic. She begins making deliveries of the stockings to stores early in September.

Parker's Painting

Parker is a house painter. He has an old truck, some ladders, scaffolding, and his tools. Sometimes he does jobs alone; other times, he hires one or two people to work with him. All of his work is done at the homes of his customers. If he needs to do a lot of work to prepare the walls and windows, he sets up a scaffold.

Wendy's Wordplay

Wendy is a self-employed writer. She works out of her home and has no employees. The only equipment she uses is her computer and printer, which she bought with a loan from her credit union.

Carly's Cooking

Carly runs a catering business. She and the people she hires do all of the cooking and serving. She has a small store with a large window which she uses for displays. She also teaches a cooking class in the window so people passing by can watch. In the back of the store she has a nicely equipped kitchen with commercial equipment.

Your Insurance Priorities

Take a few minutes to review the different kinds of insurance available to small businesses. Then, in the space below, write down which types you must have for your business.

Which other kinds of insurance would be valuable if you felt you could afford them? Check the one(s) you think are most important.

Summing Up

Take time before you start your business to decide the best form of business for you. But don't panic if you've already started selling your product or service. You can also change your choice of business form. Now that you are aware of your insurance needs, you should be able to find a good deal.

© JIST Works

CHAPTER 9

Managing Your Records

A well-designed system allows you to access vital information in a quick and timely manner. It's a must for your business. In this chapter, we review common record-keeping terms, outline how paperwork flows through a typical small business, and design a system based on that paperwork flow. Finally, at the end of the chapter you can find important IRS guidelines for maintaining your records.

Keep Your Records Well

If your business is to succeed, you need a system for recording facts and maintaining records that document your daily operations.

If your system is easy to use, you are more likely to maintain it consistently. The more complicated or cumbersome the design, the more apt you are to neglect your record-keeping. Here are some guidelines for effective record-keeping.

Guidelines for Record-Keeping

- Find an accountant with whom you are comfortable and create your system according to his or her directions.

- Make your system simple and maintain it regularly.

- Record business transactions only. Personal transactions must be separate from your business.

- Open a business checking account and use the check register to document all of your receipts (money coming in) and disbursements (money going out). Write checks to avoid making cash purchases.

- Save receipts to document all your business expenses.

- Make copies of all invoices and sales receipts issued by your business.

- Keep your business records for as long as the IRS recommends (usually three or four years, depending on the type of record).

- Store your old records in one place. Mark records according to year and record type.

- When you are in doubt about whether to keep a receipt or record a transaction, do! Ask your accountant later if it is correct.

Information Is a Management Tool

When you create and maintain a simple record-keeping system, you will always have the information you need at your fingertips. And make no mistake: You do need this information to manage your business wisely.

Don't drop all of your receipts and bills into a pile with the intention of getting to them later. The longer you wait, the more monumental the task becomes and the less likely you are to undertake it. It takes little effort to handle your documents correctly *as you receive them,* and it will save you a great deal of time, money, and aggravation in the long run.

Some business owners simply deliver a box stuffed with assorted documents to their accountants at the end of the year. They pay their accountants to read, sort, and record these documents, work they can easily perform themselves. Only at this point, after the fact, do they receive financial reports that tell them if their businesses are succeeding or failing. These owners manage their businesses in the dark, without the benefit of timely financial information.

A Simple System

The first step in creating a simple record-keeping system is to determine what information you need to manage your business. Different businesses have different information needs. A construction contractor might monitor labor and material expenses associated with an individual job to ensure that the expenses don't exceed the terms of the contract. A florist might track expenses by supplier or product type instead of by individual customers. A consultant may track billable hours by client. You must determine what your information needs are.

If you own a personal computer, consider using an accounting software program to maintain your business records. Examples of easy-to-use systems include Quicken and QuickBooks, both by Intuit, Inc. There are many other fine products available, most at reasonable prices. Before deciding on a software package, speak to your accountant or bookkeeper to determine which software package he or she uses. The process of delivery information to your accounting professional will be simpler if you use the same or compatible software.

It is a good idea to have an accounting professional assist you when you first set up your company and begin to enter transactions on a computerized system. Although most accounting software applications are very user-friendly, for that very reason, they are also quite simple to mess up if you don't know what you're doing. It is helpful to understand the fundamentals of manual record-keeping (covered in this chapter) even if you plan to use a computerized system.

Regardless of how you decide to keep your records, manually or on a personal computer, you still need to keep paper documentation of your business transactions (receipts, invoices, purchase orders, and so on). Make a list of all the paperwork you handle in your business, including documents you receive as well as those your business generates. Then draw a diagram that shows how the paperwork flows. After you do this, you can design a simple method to accommodate your paperwork flow.

Common Record-Keeping Terms

- **Accounts payable/Trade payable:** Money you owe to your regular business creditors. Unpaid amounts are **open accounts payable.** After they have been paid, they are **closed accounts payable.**

- **Accounts receivable/Trade receivable:** Money owed to you by your customers. Unpaid amounts are **open accounts receivable.** After they have been paid, they are **closed accounts receivable.**

- **Cash sales:** Sales made to customers when no credit has been extended. Cash sales are paid for at the time the sale is made and are documented with a **cash sale receipt.**

- **Cash receipts:** Any receipt of money. A cash receipt occurs both when a customer pays your accounts receivable (credit was extended) and when a customer pays a cash sale (no credit was extended). The term can be misleading, since it can represent cash, checks, and credit card sales.

- **Credit memo:** A reduction or credit applied against a previously issued invoice. Credit memos can be a result of shipping errors, price reductions, damaged goods, returns, or canceled orders. Credit memos have unique identifying numbers.

- **Debit memo:** An increase or debit applied against a previously issued invoice. Debit memos can be a result of original invoice errors, price adjustments, or order add-ons. Debit memos have unique identifying numbers.

- **Invoice:** A bill sent from a creditor to a customer. Invoices have payment terms consistent with the type of account the customer has with the creditor. Invoices have unique identifying numbers.

- **Invoice terms:** Payment agreement a creditor extends to a customer. Common invoice terms include these:
  - **COD:** Cash on delivery
  - **Due upon receipt:** Payment due upon receipt of invoice
  - **Net 10, Net 15, Net 30:** The number of days (10, 15, 30, etc.) before payment in full is due
  - **2/10 Net/30:** 2 percent discount can be taken if paid within 10 days, or full payment is due in 30 days

- **Packing slip:** Document a business encloses with a shipment to a customer. The packing slip verifies the contents of the shipment and compares it to the customer's order. Packing slips reference the customer's purchase order number, if applicable, and contain all relevant shipping information. Packing slips have unique identifying numbers.

- **Purchase order:** Form a business uses to place an order with a creditor. Purchase orders (POs) specify the buyer's name, account number, billing address, shipping address, and order details. POs have unique identifying numbers.

Fiona's Photos

Fiona is a photographer who specializes in weddings. She has just started her own business, *Fiona's Photos.* Fiona wants a record-keeping system that will keep her organized. Since she has worked for a photography studio for many years, Fiona knows what is reasonable to expect from customers and suppliers. Here is Fiona's plan:

Before she is hired to photograph a wedding, Fiona will schedule an initial consultation with the clients. During this consultation, Fiona and the clients will review samples of her work as well as her price sheet. Fiona and the clients will agree on a price based on how many rolls of film she is expected to shoot and how many hours she will remain at the wedding. Fiona will prepare a contract that both she and the clients will sign. The cost of shooting the wedding will be paid in full before the wedding date, when Fiona will give the clients a cash sale receipt (#1 in the following figure).

Fiona will order film from her supplier using a purchase order form. She will receive the film along with a packing slip verifying the contents of the shipment. The following week, the supplier will send an invoice for the film. After the wedding, Fiona will send the film to a photo lab so proofs can be developed. She will send a purchase order with the film so the lab knows what she wants. The lab will return the proofs with a packing slip. A week later, she will receive an invoice for the proofs.

After the proofs are developed, the clients will choose how many and what size finished photos they will purchase. Fiona will collect a 60 percent deposit from the clients before she places the final order with the photo lab. She'll give the clients another cash sale receipt (#2) for this deposit. Fiona will order the photos on a purchase order form. After the pictures are developed, the lab will send them to Fiona with a packing slip and an invoice. Fiona will collect the 40 percent balance due from the clients when they pick up their wedding pictures. She'll make a notation on the cash sale receipt (#2) that the order has been paid in full.

Below is a list of the documents Fiona needs in her record-keeping system.

Fiona's Documents

Type of Document	Generated By	Document Use
Customer contract	Fiona	Enter into initial agreement with client
Cash sale receipt	Fiona	Collect shooting fee from client
Purchase order	Fiona	Place order to purchase film from supplier
Packing slip	Film supplier	Delivered with film shipment to verify order
Invoice	Film supplier	Pay supplier for film
Purchase order	Fiona	Order proofs from developing lab
Packing slip	Photo lab	Delivered with proofs to verify order
Invoice	Photo lab	Pay photo lab for proofs
Cash sale receipt	Fiona	Started when 60 percent deposit is collected and completed when 40 percent balance is collected
Purchase order	Fiona	Sent to photo lab to place picture order
Packing slip	Photo lab	Delivered with photos to verify picture order
Invoice	Photo lab	Pay photo lab for picture order

© JIST Works

When Fiona drew a picture of her paperwork flow, it looked like this:

Before Fiona can organize her record-keeping system, she needs to determine what information is important to her business. For example, when Fiona accesses a client's file, she wants all the information about all the work she performed for that client. Fiona also wants to be able to pull a supplier's file and see how much business she has done with that company. She needs quick access to her outstanding accounts receivable and accounts payable balances.

Her system must be organized so that she can determine if her purchase orders were filled correctly. She will need to verify that she received a product before she pays an invoice for it. Fiona needs to organize open accounts payable so she'll know when it's time to pay a bill—not too early and not too late. She also wants to record all her transactions in one place so that she can tell at a glance how well she is managing her money.

Here is the system Fiona designed to meet her needs:

1. **When Fiona begins working with a new client, she creates a *Client File.*** On the file label she includes the client's name and the date the file was created. She keeps a data sheet inside the folder that includes the client's name, address, and phone number and how he or she heard about Fiona. In this folder, Fiona files the original, executed contract she and the client have both signed. She staples a few sheets of blank paper to the inside of this file folder. On this paper, she records dates and notes of conversations and meetings and all action she takes regarding this client.

2. **She creates a single file folder labeled *Accounts Receivable Control File.*** Each time Fiona issues an invoice (she uses the same numbered invoices for credit customers and cash sales), she files copy #1 here in numerical order. This is a permanent control file.

3. **If an invoice Fiona issued was for a cash sale, she stamps copy #2 paid and indicates the date, check number, and amount of payment.** She then files the paid invoice in the appropriate client file. If the invoice is not paid at the time of issue, copy #2 is filed in a single folder she has labeled Open Accounts Receivable. The invoice remains here until Fiona receives payment. When it has been paid, Fiona removes the invoice from the file; marks it paid; records the date, check number, and payment amount; and files it in the client's file.

4. **Fiona labels a single file folder *Purchase Orders Control File.*** She keeps copy #1 of every PO she writes in this file in numerical order. This is a permanent control file.

5. **Fiona also labels a single file folder *Open Purchase Orders.*** Each time she writes a purchase order, she files copy #2 in this file, where it remains as long as the PO is open. Each time a shipment comes in, Fiona matches the packing slip against the open purchase order. If there is a problem, Fiona calls her supplier immediately to resolve it. If there are no discrepancies, Fiona staples them together and returns them both to the *Open Purchase Orders* file.

6. **Fiona has an accordion file folder with 31 slots numbered for the days of the month.** She labels this folder *Open Accounts Payable.* Each day that she gets an invoice from a supplier, she matches the invoice against her purchase order and the packing slip (she finds these already stapled together in the *Open Purchase Orders* file). This way, she is certain she received a complete order before she pays the invoice. If everything matches, she staples the invoice to the supporting documents. Next, she checks the invoice due date. She determines the date she will need to write a check and mail it so that the payment will arrive on time. She files the invoice in *Open Accounts Payable* under the correct date. Fiona also files all other bills here, including utility, insurance, and tax bills.

   Each day, Fiona looks in the *Open Accounts Payable* file and pays the bills that are in the slot for that date. After she pays the bill, she writes the date, the check number, and the amount paid on the invoice. She stamps the invoice *paid* with a red rubber stamp.

7. **Fiona has another accordion file folder, but this one has 26 slots designated A through Z.** She labels this folder *Closed Accounts Payable.* Each time Fiona pays an invoice, she files the paid invoice here alphabetically by the creditor's name.

© *JIST Works*

Here you can see a diagram of Fiona's record-keeping system. Compare it to the diagram Fiona drew earlier and you will see how Fiona's record-keeping system accommodates her natural flow of paperwork.

- Using this system, **Fiona can easily see how much money her clients owe her** by looking in the *Open Accounts Receivable* file and adding the invoice amounts.

- **She will always know how much money she owes her creditors** by looking in the *Open Accounts Payable* file.

- **She will know when her bills need to be paid** because they are sorted by the days of the month. This will save Fiona time when she is preparing cash-flow projections each month.

- **Fiona can see how much she has spent with any one supplier** by looking in the *Closed Accounts Payable* file, where she will find all of their paid invoices.

- By looking in the *Open Purchase Orders* file, **Fiona can see if she has placed any orders that have not been fulfilled.**

- Fiona created two control files where invoice and PO copies are filed numerically. The control files allow her to look these up quickly by their identifying numbers. Documents in control files are never removed, so **Fiona has a permanent record of every invoice and PO her business issues.**

- In designing this system, Fiona has discovered that **her contract forms require at least two copies:** one for Fiona to keep in the client's file and one to give to her clients.

- She learned that **her invoices will require at least three copies.** The first she will give to the customer. The second copy she will file numerically in the *Accounts Receivable Control File.* The third will go in *Open Accounts Receivable* before it is paid and then move to the *Client File* after it is paid.

- **Fiona's purchase orders need at least three copies.** The first will be sent to the supplier to place an order. The second will be filed numerically in the *Purchase Order Control File*. The third will begin in *Open Purchase Orders* before the order is received. After the order has been received and invoiced, it will move to *Open Accounts Payable*. After the invoice has been paid, it will land in *Closed Accounts Payable*.

Posting to Journals

The last thing Fiona needs to add to her record-keeping system is a place to record her transactions. Businesses use *journals* to record financial transactions. Journals document events in chronological order. When a transaction has been recorded in a journal, it has been *posted*. A business can choose to post transactions to a *cash journal* or to a *general journal*.

In cash journals, only cash transactions are recorded. When cash sales are made and the money is deposited in the bank account or when checks are written to pay expenses, they are recorded in the cash journal. Accounts receivable and accounts payable are not recorded in cash journals until they are paid. Only when cash has been received from customers or paid to creditors are the transactions recorded. Cash journals are simple to maintain, but they provide a limited amount of information.

General journals record all financial transactions—cash transactions as well as accounts receivable and accounts payable. With a general journal, a business owner can tell at a glance where money comes from, where money is going, how much money is owed to creditors, and how much money customers owe the business. A general journal gives the owner a more accurate picture of the business.

Journals should be delivered to an accountant for periodic review. The accountant can then generate financial reports quickly, which saves the business owner a great deal of money in accounting fees, since the accountant works from the journal instead of from boxes of paperwork.

Manual journals can be created using columnar pads (available in most office supply stores—see the example in this section). If a business owns a personal computer, many computerized accounting packages are available that make record-keeping easy. Journals also can be created on personal computers by using spreadsheet programs.

On the following pages you will find an exercise and examples of both cash and general journals.

© JIST Works

Columnar Pads

This is an example of a four-column columnar pad. These pads are available with 2 to 24 (or more) "currency" columns per page.

The column on the far left is used to enter the transaction date. The wide column is used to describe the transaction. The four currency columns on the right are marked so the user can easily enter dollars and cents.

Exercise #1

In accounting, every transaction has at least two sides: one entry balanced with an equal and opposite entry. For example, when you pay the rent, you aren't just paying the rent, you disburse money from the bank to pay the rent. To record the transaction, you post one entry to the bank account and another entry to the rent expense account. Here are some examples of two sides of transactions:

	Post Entry #1 to:	Post Entry #2 to:
1. Make a cash sale:	Bank Account ($ deposited)	Sales Income (sale posted)
2. Pay owner's salary:	Bank Account ($ disbursed)	Salary Expense (expense posted)
3. Receive a business loan:	Bank Account ($ deposited)	Loan Payable (loan posted)

A business creates a chart of accounts to identify and number the accounts used in their accounting system. Based on the following chart of accounts, see if you can identify the "missing side" of each business transaction below.

Chart of Accounts

101 Checking Account
400 Sales Income
401 Misc. Income
500 Accounting
502 Automobile Expenses
505 Dues & Subscriptions
508 Depreciation
510 Fees: Bank Charges & Misc.
515 Insurance: Business
516 Insurance: Health
520 Interest Expense
525 Labor: Payroll Expense
526 Labor: Employee Benefits
530 Materials
545 Miscellaneous
550 Owner's Compensation
560 Repair & Maintenance
570 Taxes
580 Utilities

1. Employee health insurance premiums are paid.

   Entry 1: **516, Insurance: Health** (expense posted)

   Entry 2: _____

2. Gasoline expenses are reimbursed to employees.

   Entry 1: **101, Checking Account** ($ disbursed)

   Entry 2: _____

3. A customer pays cash for a purchase.

   Entry 1: **101, Checking Account** ($ deposited)

   Entry 2: _____

4. The gas bill is paid.

   Entry 1: **101, Checking Account** ($ disbursed)

   Entry 2: _____

5. The bank deducts a monthly fee directly from the checking account.

   Entry 1: **510, Fees: Bank Charges & Misc.** (expense posted)

   Entry 2: _____

© JIST Works

The Cash Journal

The simplest journal to keep is a cash journal. Entries posted to this journal are based on the movement of cash in and out of the business checking account. The checkbook register is the primary source of information for a cash journal. The cash journal describes the sources of cash coming in and the uses of cash going out.

In the example that follows, column 1 is used to record transaction dates. Column 2 is used to describe each transaction. Column 3 is to record check numbers. Columns 4 and 5 are for the *Bank Account Cash In* and *Cash Out*. Next is a column for invoice numbers. Sales income is recorded in column 7. In columns 8 and 9, any other sources of cash in are described and posted. The remaining columns (10 through 16) are for commonly used operating expenses (film, proofs, photos, rent, and utilities). The last two columns are for any other cash out transactions and expenses that don't occur often enough to require their own column.

Each time a deposit is made into the business checking account (lines 2 and 4), it is recorded in the *Bank Account Cash In,* column 4. If the source of the deposit is a sale, the sale amount is recorded in the *Sales Income,* column 7. Sometimes deposits come from other sources, such as an owner's investment or loan proceeds. These amounts are described in column 8 and recorded in column 9 (line 1).

When a check is written, it is posted in *Bank Account Cash Out,* column 5. A corresponding entry is made in the expense account columns (lines 3 and 5) or column 16, *Other Cash Out* (line 6).

At the end of the month, the columns are totaled. To determine if all entries are posted correctly, the cash journal is balanced as follows:

1. Total Cash In (column 4) = Total Income + Other Cash In (column 7 + 8)

2. Total Cash Out (column 5) = Total Expenses + Other Cash Out (columns 10 through 16)

An imbalance indicates that an entry is improperly posted or there is a mathematical error. You can perform the following calculations after the journal has been balanced:

1. Subtract *Cash Out* from *Cash In* to get the bank balance. This balance should agree with the checkbook register.

2. To determine if a profit was made or a loss sustained, subtract *Total Expenses* (columns 10 through 16) from *Total Income* (column 7).

It's easy to identify how much money is being spent in each category. Compare these to the cash-flow projections made at the beginning of the month. Is the amount of sales income as high as or higher than projected for the month? By providing historical data, cash journal totals can be used to improve future cash-flow projections.

Fiona's Photo Studio - CASH JOURNAL

1	2	3	BANK ACCOUNT		6	7	OTHER CASH IN		10	11	12	13	14	OTHER EXPENSES + CASH OUT	
Date Jan 2XXX	Description	Check Number	CASH IN	CASH OUT	Invoice Number	SALES INCOME	DESCRIPTION	AMOUNT	FILM EXPENSE	PROOFS EXPENSE	PHOTOS EXPENSE	RENT EXPENSE	UTIL EXPENSE	DESCRIPTION	AMOUNT
01/01	Open Bank Account		$1,000.00				OWNER INVEST	$1,000.00							
01/01	Jones Sale-INV #101		$250.00		100	$250.00									
01/01	ABC Landlord RENT	1001		$300.00								$300.00			
01/04	Smith - Sale-INV #102		$50.00		101	$50.00									
01/31	Film, Inc.	1002		$25.00					$25.00						
01/31	Mark-Owner's Comp	1003		$125.00										SALARY	$125.00
	Totals This Month		$1,300.00	$450.00		$300.00		$1,000.00	$25.00	$0.00	$0.00	$300.00	$0.00		$125.00
	Bank Balance:		$850.00			$1,300.00						$450.00			

*Ending balances this month become beginning balances next month

Income $300.00   Cash In = $1,300.00 / $1,300.00   Income + Other cash in =

Expenses $450.00   Cash Out = $450.00 / $450.00   All Expenses + Other cash out =

Profit/Loss: ($150.00)

Cash Journal Is in Balance

© JIST Works

The General Journal

General journals require a little more work than cash journals. However, if your business has accounts receivable (A/R) and/or accounts payable (A/P), general journals give a more accurate accounting of your business.

In a general journal, A/P expenses and A/R income are recognized as they are incurred, not when they are paid. This means that you post an expense when you receive an invoice, not when you pay the invoice. You post a sale when you issue the invoice to the customer, not when the customer pays the invoice.

Consider the importance of this: If your business ceased operations today, your customers would still owe you for accounts receivable issued, and you would still be responsible to your creditors for accounts payable received. They reflect events that have already taken place. The general journal provides an up-to-date picture of your business because it always includes your A/R and A/P.

There is a general journal example on the next page. The general journal design is similar to the cash journal, but it includes *Accounts Receivable Issued* (column 10) and *Accounts Receivable Paid* (column 11). It also includes *Accounts Payable Received* (column 13) and *Accounts Payable Paid* (column 12).

Take a look at how A/R and A/P entries are posted to the general journal. When an invoice is issued to a customer (line 2), an entry is made under *Sales Income* (column 7) and *A/R Issued* (column 10). When the customer pays the invoice (line 7), an entry is made under *Bank Account Cash In* (column 4) and under *A/R Paid* (column 11).

When an invoice is received from a supplier (line 6), an entry is posted under *A/P Received* (column 13), and the corresponding expense account, *Film* (column 14). When the invoice is paid (line 9), an entry is made under *Bank Account Cash Out* (column 5) and under *A/P Paid* (column 12).

At the end of the month, the columns are totaled. Balancing a general journal is a little more complex than balancing a cash journal, since there are more columns. (Your accountant can help you design and balance your general journal.) These are the columns you add in this general journal to balance:

Balancing:

Bank Cash In		Bank Cash Out
A/R Issued		A/R Paid
A/P Paid		A/P Rec'd
All Expenses		Sales Income
+ Other Cash Out		+ Other Cash In
Totals	=	Totals

Fiona's Photo Studio - GENERAL JOURNAL

Date Jan 2XXX	Description	Check #	Bank Account Cash In	Bank Account Cash Out	Invoice #	Sales Income Amount	Other Cash In Descrip	Other Cash In Amount	Accts Receivable Issued	Accts Receivable (Paid)	Accts Payable Paid	Accts Payable (Received)	Film Expense	Proofs Expense	Photos Expense	Rent Expense	Util Expense	Other Exp + Cash Out Descrip	Other Exp + Cash Out Amount
01/01	Open Bank Account		$1,000.00				OWNER INVEST	$1,000.00											
01/01	Jones Sale (A/R Issued)				100	$250.00			$250.00										
01/01	ABC Landlord (Rent)	1001		$300.00												$300.00			
01/02	Lawson Wedding				101	$100.00			$100.00										
01/04	Smith Cash Sale		$50.00		102	$50.00													
01/12	Film, Inc. (A/P Rec'd)											$25.00	$25.00						
01/15	Jones (A/R Paid)		$250.00							$250.00									
01/16	The Photo Lab, Inc.											$415.00			$415.00				
01/31	Film, Inc. (A/P Pd.)	1002		$25.00							$25.00								
01/31	Mark - Salary	1003		$125.00														Salary	$125.00
	Totals This Month		$1,300.00	$450.00		$400.00		$1,000.00	$350.00	$250.00	$25.00	$440.00	$25.00	$0.00	$415.00	$300.00	$0.00		$125.00
	Account Balances:		$865.00						$100.00			$415.00				$865.00			

*Ending balances this month become beginning balances next month

Bank Cash In	$1,300.00
Accts Receivable Issued	350.00
Accts Payables Paid	$25.00
All Expenses + Other Cash Out	$865.00
	$2,540.00
Bank Cash Out	$450.00
Accts Receivable Paid	$250.00
Accts Payable Rec'd	$440.00
All Income + Other Cash In	$1,400.00
	$2,540.00

General Journal in Balance

Acct Rec Balance:	$100.00
Acct Pay Balance:	$415.00
Bank Balance:	$850.00
Income:	$400.00
Expenses:	$865.00
Profit (loss):	($465.00)

© JIST Works

Fiona's Photo Studio – GENERAL JOURNAL MONTH #2

			BANK ACCOUNT			SALES INCOME	OTHER CASH IN		ACCTS RECEIVABLE		ACCTS PAYABLE		FILM	PROOFS	PHOTOS	RENT	UTIL	OTHER EXPENSES + CASH OUT	
Date Jan 2XXX	Description	Check #	CASH IN	CASH OUT	Invoice #	AMOUNT	DESCRIP	AMOUNT	ISSUED	(PAID)	PAID	(RECEIVED)	EXPENSE	EXPENSE	EXPENSE	EXPENSE	EXPENSE	DESCRIP	AMOUNT
	Beginning Balances:		$1,300.00	$450.00		$400.00		$1,000.00	$350.00	$250.00	$25.00	$440.00	$25.00	$0.00	$415.00	$300.00	$0.00		$125.00
02/01	ABC Landlord (Rent)	1004		$300.00												$300.00			
02/01	Kennedy–Cash Sale		$150.00		103	$150.00													
02/15	Walters – (A/R Issued)				104	$400.00			$400.00										
02/28	Film, Inc.											$25.00	$25.00						
	MTD Totals:		$150.00	$300.00		$550.00		$0.00	$400.00	$0.00	$0.00	$25.00	$25.00	$0.00	$0.00	$300.00	$0.00		$0.00
																$325.00			
	YTD Totals:		$1,450.00	$750.00		$950.00		$1,000.00	$750.00	$250.00	$25.00	$465.00	$50.00	$0.00	$415.00	$600.00	$0.00		$125.00
	YTD Acct Balances:		$700.00						$500.00			$440.00				$1,190.00			

Bank Cash In $150.00 $1,450.00
Accts Receivable Issued $400.00 $750.00
Accts Payables Paid $0.00 $25.00
All Expenses + Other Cash Out $325.00 $1,190.00
   $875.00 $3,415.00

Bank Cash Out $450.00 $750.00
Accts Receivable Paid $0.00 $250.00
Accts Payable Rec'd $25.00 $465.00
All Income + Other Cash In $550.00 $1,950.00
   $875.00 $3,415.00

Acct Rec Balance: $500.00
Acct Pay Balance: $440.00
Bank Balance: $700.00

MTD Income: $550.00
MTD Expenses: $325.00
MTD Profit (loss): $225.00

YTD Income: $950.00
YTD Expenses: $1,190.00
YTD Profit (loss): ($240.00)

General Journal Is in Balance

In the example, you can look at the totals in *A/R Issued and A/R Paid* and see that more invoices were issued than paid. By subtracting *A/R Paid* from *A/R Issued,* you get the current outstanding *A/R Balance:* $100.

The total *A/P Received* is $440 and the total *A/P Paid* was $25. By subtracting $25 from $440, you get the current outstanding *A/P Balance:* $415.

Calculate the ending bank balance by subtracting cash out from cash in. Determine profit or loss by subtracting total expenses from sales income.

On page 113, you'll find an example of a general journal for the following month. Notice that prior month ending balances become beginning balances and year-to-date balances are calculated.

General Information

The following section deals with how long you should keep documents, questions you should ask when interviewing an accountant, and Internal Revenue Service publications and guidelines.

How Long to Keep Your Records

- Keep all business records for at least three years from the date the tax return was due or filed or two years from the date the tax was paid, whichever occurs later.

- Keep asset records that verify your basis in property for as long as they are needed to figure the basis of the original or replacement property and/or figure investment credit or recapture. *Basis* is the original cost of an item plus additional out-of-pocket costs, such as the cost of improvements.

- You may need to keep some records for an indefinite period to support decisions regarding changes in accounting methods or inventory valuations.

- If you are an employer, retain all records and returns pertaining to employment taxes, such as income tax withholding, Social Security taxes, and federal unemployment taxes, for at least four years after the due date of the return or four years after the date the tax was paid, whichever is later.

IRS Publication 15, *Employers Tax Guide* (Circular E), is the primary reference for an employer. Additional information and methods for special cases can be found in IRS Publication 493, *Alternative Tax Withholding Methods and Tables.*

© JIST Works

Exercise #2

Post the following transactions to the ABC Co.'s general ledger below.

2/1: ABC Co. makes a $25 cash sale to Mrs. Meyer.

2/2: Invoice #252 is issued to Mr. Klien for a $50 purchase.

2/2: ABC Co. receives a $30 invoice from The Office Store for file folders purchased.

2/9: ABC Co. writes check #101 to The Office Store for a $10 cash purchase of pencils.

2/28: Mr. Klien pays ABC Co. $30 against invoice #252.

Total the transactions, balance the general ledger, and fill in the blanks.

	1	2	3	4	5	6	7	8	9	10	11	12	
	Date Feb 2XXX	Description	Check #	BANK ACCOUNT CASH IN	CASH OUT	Invoice #	SALES INCOME	Accts Receivable Issued	Paid	Accts Payable Paid	Received	Ofc Supply EXPENSE	
1		Beg. Balances:		$300.00	$145.00		$300.00	$100.00	$100.00	$145.00	$200.00	$200.00	1
2													2
3													3
4													4
5													5
6													6
7													7
8		MTD Totals:											8
9													9
10		YTD Totals:											10
11													11
12													12
13		YTD Account Balances:											13

	YTD:		YTD:
Bank Cash In		A/R Bal:	
Accts Receivable Issued		A/P Bal:	
Accts Payable Paid		Bank Bal:	
Expenses			
Total:			

Bank Cash Out		Income:	
Accts Receivable Paid		Expense:	
Accts Payable Rec'd		Profit (loss):	
Income			
Total:		Is ABC Co. Profitable?	

Is Journal in Balance?

Suggested IRS Publications

The following publications can be obtained through your local IRS office:

Publication Number	Title
15	Employers Tax Guide (Circular E)
17	Your Federal Income Tax
334	Tax Guide for Small Business
454	Your Business Tax Kit
463	Travel, Entertainment, Gift, and Car Expense
493	Alternative Tax W/H Methods & Tables
505	Tax Withholding & Estimated Tax
525	Taxable & Nontaxable Income
533	Self-Employment Tax
534	Depreciation
535	Business Expenses
539	Employment Taxes & Information Returns
541	Tax Information on Partnerships
542	Tax Information on Corporations
551	Basis for Assets
560	Retirement Plans for Small Business
583	Starting a Business and Keeping Records
587	Business Use of Your Home (Including Use by Day Care Providers)
589	Tax Information on S Corporations
1057	Intro to Federal Taxes for Small Business/Self Employed
1518	Small Business Tax Calendar
1853	Small Business Talk
3207	Small Business Resource Guide: What You Need to Know About Taxes and Other Topics
3700	Virtual Small Business Workshop

The IRS and other federal agencies provide assistance to business owners. For more information, contact your local IRS office Monday through Friday during normal business hours and ask to speak with the Taxpayer Education Coordinator. Call the IRS at 1-800-829-1040. You can also access the IRS on the Internet at http://www.irs.gov. Tax forms can be ordered through the IRS Web site, or you can receive forms and instructions by calling 1-703-368-9694 using a phone attached to a fax machine (you will need to know the publication or catalog number of the forms you would like to receive).

© JIST Works

Selecting an Accountant

Here is a list of questions you should ask when you are interviewing accountants:

- Can you provide me with some client references from other businesses in my field?
- How are your fees structured?
- How often will we meet?
- What can I do to reduce your workload (and thus your fees)?
- Are you qualified to discuss my business's tax requirements?
- Will you review and advise me regarding my record-keeping?
- What are your office hours?
- Is there a staff member available when you are not?
- How quickly will my financial reports be generated and delivered?
- May I have an engagement letter that details our agreement?

Employee or Independent Contractor?

According to the IRS, an employer generally must withhold income taxes, withhold and pay Social Security and Medicare taxes, and pay unemployment taxes on wages paid to an employee. An employer generally does not have to withhold or pay taxes on payments to independent contractors.

To help you determine whether an individual is an employee under the common-law rules, the IRS has identified some guidelines to determine whether sufficient control is present to establish an employer-employee relationship. These are only guidelines. It does not matter if you have a written agreement stating that certain factors do not apply if the facts indicate otherwise. If an employer makes an incorrect determination and treats an employee as an independent contractor, the employer could be held personally liable for an amount equal to the taxes that should have been withheld.

The common-law rules based on the relationship between the worker and the business will help you determine if an individual is an employee or an independent contractor. These rules include:

- Behavioral Control: Facts that show whether the business has the right to direct and control how the worker does the task for which the worker is hired include the type and degree of
  - Instructions the business gives the worker (when and where to do the work, what tools to use, what workers to hire or assist with the work, where to purchase supplies and services, what work must be performed by a specific individual, what order or sequence to follow).
  - Training the business gives the worker. An employee may be trained to perform services in a particular manner. Independent contractors ordinarily use their own methods.

- Financial Control: Facts that show whether the business has a right to control the business aspects of the worker's job, including
  - The extent to which the worker has unreimbursed business expenses.
  - The extent of the worker's investment.
  - The extent to which the worker makes services available to the general market (other than the business in question).
  - How the business pays the worker.
  - The extent to which the worker can realize a profit or loss.
- Type of relationship: Facts that show the parties' relationship include
  - Written contracts describing the relationship the parties intended to create.
  - Whether the business provides the worker with employee-type benefits (insurance, pension plan, sick pay, vacation pay).
  - The permanency of the relationship.
  - The extent to which services performed by the worker are a key aspect of the regular business of the company.

For more information, request IRS publication 15A. To have the IRS help you determine if a worker is an employee, file Form SS-8, "Determination of Employee Work Status for Purpose of Federal Employment Taxes and Income Tax Withholding."

Summing Up

An effective record-keeping system is a must for your small business. A well-designed system is simple and easy to use and allows you to access important information quickly. Whether you choose to create a manual record-keeping system or use a personal computer and small business accounting software, it will be helpful to first understand the fundamentals of manual record-keeping. Consider what information you need to manage your business, what paperwork your business generates, and what documents you receive as you design your system. Don't be afraid to consult a bookkeeper or an accountant familiar with your type of business to assist you in setting up your system.

© JIST Works

CHAPTER 10

Understanding Financial Statements

In this chapter, you learn to read financial statements. Successful business owners use financial reports as vital management tools. Most small businesses don't generate their own financials, but all small business owners should understand how to read them.

After you understand the components of financial statements, you'll have the chance to examine the effect different management decisions have on similar businesses. You'll also learn what lenders look for when analyzing financial reports.

Just the Facts, Ma'am

Who uses financial statements? What do they tell about a business? How often should they be generated? Most importantly, why bother? You find out in this section.

Who?

Financial statements are used by many people, but none more important than the business owner. Successful business owners use financial statements as management tools. They refer to these reports on a regular basis to make daily operating decisions. And before they make any critical business decision, they examine their financial reports.

Some business owners believe that financial statements are for accountants and bankers. They pay an accountant to generate the statements and then send copies to the bank. They rely on their accountant to read the reports and alert them to any problems. By doing this, they relinquish some control of their businesses and rely on chance that everything will be all right.

What?

Financial statements consist of two primary elements: the balance sheet and the income statement. When people ask for financial statements, sometimes they also want other reports, such as cash-flow statements or projections.

When?

How often financial statements should be generated and reviewed depends on the size and type of business. Some businesses need only quarterly financial reports, but most businesses are better served with monthly reports. If your record-keeping system includes an up-to-date general journal, you already have considerable financial information on a daily basis. Your accountant can help you determine what best suits your information needs.

Why?

Operating a business without financial statements is like driving a car blindfolded. You wouldn't know when (or if) you reached your destination—and that would be the least of your problems. More important, you couldn't see obstacles in your way, and you wouldn't know if you were in danger until it was too late. You couldn't see what you were doing right or where you were going off course. You could get hurt because of your recklessness, and so could others. Driving blindfolded is not smart. Whether driving a car or running a business, you need to see where you've been, where you are, and where you're going.

Before you can use your financial statement as a management tool, you must first understand how to read it.

You Ought to Be in Pictures!

Financial statements are pictures of your business that serve two important functions:

1. The balance sheet reports the net worth of the business.
2. The income statement reports how the business is being operated.

The Balance Sheet

The balance sheet is a financial snapshot of your business at a given point in time. It tells you, as of a specific date, several important things:

- What your business owns
- The debt for which your business is liable
- The net worth of your business

The information is categorized as follows:

- Assets (what you own)
- Liabilities (what you owe)
- Equity (your net worth)

Since a balance sheet is a financial picture taken on a specific date, it is labeled as such: Balance sheet for ABC Company, Inc., as of XX/XX/XXXX

The Income Statement

Your income statement is a financial movie that covers a specific period of time. It tells you if your business operated at a profit or suffered a loss during a specific period of time.

This information is categorized as follows:

- Income (revenue generated)
- Expenses (cost of operations)
- Profit or loss (difference between income and expenses)

Since an income statement covers a specific period, it is labeled as such: Income Statement for ABC Company, Inc., for the period ending XX/XX/XXXX

© JIST Works

Exercise #1

Perhaps the easiest way to understand financial statements is to examine a set. In this exercise, we identify an asset, liability, equity, income, and expense item and indicate whether each is found on the balance sheet or income statement.

Month #1	Description	Balance Sheet/ Income Statement
Mary's take-home pay from her job is $2,000 per month.	Income	Income Statement
Her living expenses total $1,500 per month.	Expenses	Income Statement
The difference between her income and expenses is $500.	Profit (Loss)	Income Statement
Mary puts her monthly "profit" into a savings account.	Asset	Balance Sheet
Mary just bought a car for $6,000.	Asset	Balance Sheet
She put $1,000 down to buy the car.	Equity	Balance Sheet
Mary has an auto loan with a balance of $5,000.	Liability	Balance Sheet
Mary is buying a house; the purchase price is $45,000.	Asset	Balance Sheet
She put $5,000 down on the house.	Equity	Balance Sheet
She has a mortgage loan balance of $40,000.	Liability	Balance Sheet

Mary's Balance Sheet as of 1/31/2XXX

Assets

Bank Balance	$500
House	$45,000
Car	$6,000
Assets:	**$51,500**

Liabilities

Mortgage loan	$40,000
Car loan	$5,000
Liabilities:	**$45,000**

Equity (net worth)

Home equity:	$5,000
Car equity:	$1,000
Profit (Loss)	$500
Equity:	**$6,500**

Total Assets:	**$51,500**
Total Liabilities & Equity:	**$51,500**

Mary's Income Statement as of 1/31/2XXX

Income

Salary	$2,000

Expenses

Mortgage Payment	$500
Food	$200
Utilities	$300
Insurance	$100
Car Payment	$300
Miscellaneous	$100
Total Expenses	**$1,500**
Profit (Loss)	**$500**

Is This Picture in Focus?

Take a closer look at some examples of *assets, liabilities,* and *equity:*

- David buys a car for $5,000. He puts $ 1,000 down and takes out a car loan for $4,000.

Asset (what you own)	Automobile	$5,000
Liability (what you owe)	Auto loan	$4,000
Equity (net worth)	Auto equity	$1,000

- Kathy buys a house for $40,000. Her down payment is $5,000. Her mortgage is $35,000.

Asset (what you own)	Home	$40,000
Liability (what you owe)	Mortgage	$35,000
Equity (net worth)	Home equity	$5,000

- James has a savings account balance of $2,000. He has credit card debt of $1,800.

Asset (what you own)	Savings account	$2,000
Liability (what you owe)	Credit card debt	$1,800
Equity (net worth)	Net worth	$200

Looking at the examples above, you will notice that there is a common equation:

Assets – Liabilities = Equity

Another way to write this same equation is as follows:

Assets = Liabilities + Equity

Let's test this and see if it works.

	Assets – Liabilities = Equity	**or**	**Assets = Liabilities + Equity**
David:	$5,000 – $4,000 = $1,000	or	$5,000 = $4,000 + $1,000
Kathy:	$40,000 – $35,000 = $5,000	or	$40,000 = $35,000 + $5,000
James:	$2,000 – $1,800 = $200	or	$2,000 = $1,800 + $200

Assets = Liabilities + Equity is *the* fundamental accounting equation. Balance sheets are so called because they are designed to balance using this equation. Following is an example of a balance sheet.

David's Balance Sheet as of 1/31/2XXX

Assets		**Liabilities**	
Automobile	$5,000	Auto loan	$4,000
		Equity	
		Auto equity	$1,000
Total Assets:	$5,000	**Total Liabilities & Equity:**	$5,000

© *JIST Works*

The Whole Family Album

Income statements describe operating income and expenses over a period of time (for example, one month). If a business generates more income than expense, it earns a profit. If a business incurs more expense than income, it suffers a loss.

We know that balance sheets report the net worth (equity) of a business and that income statements report profit or loss. If a business is profitable, doesn't that increase its equity? If a business is suffering a loss, doesn't that decrease its equity? If so, then doesn't the profit or loss of the income statement need to be reflected on the balance sheet?

The answer is yes. Profit or loss is taken directly from the income statement and recorded on the balance sheet in an equity account called *retained earnings*. In the following example, you can see how this happens.

ABC Widgets

ABC Widgets is owned by Mr. I.M. Good. Mr. Good started his business with an initial investment of $5,000.

Here is Mr. Good's opening balance sheet:

Balance Sheet for ABC Widgets as of 1/1/2XXX

Assets		Liabilities	
Bank account	$5,000	Accounts payable	$0
Accounts receivable	$0		
Inventory	$0	**Equity**	
Equipment	$0	Owner's equity	$5,000
		Retained earnings	$0
		Total Equity	**$5,000**
Total Assets	**$5,000**	**Liabilities & Equity**	**$5,000**

Mr. Good started his business with $5,000 of his personal savings. His investment in his business is recorded as *equity* in an account called *owner's equity*. The $5,000 balance will remain unless Mr. Good reduces or increases his investment into his business. Mr. Good deposited the cash in the *bank account*. The opening balance sheet is in balance.

Mr. Good decided to market his new business aggressively. His decision to spend money on advertising has paid off. Sales are above Mr. Good's projections, and he has made a net profit of $570. Here is Mr. Good's first income statement:

Mr. Good collected $4,700 in widget sales. That income was deposited into the bank account. He also paid $1,645 in COGS and $2,485 in fixed expenses. By the end of the month, his bank balance was $5,570. The balance sheet reflects this new bank balance.

ABC Widgets earned a profit of $570. This amount is recorded as *equity, retained earnings.*

Below is the balance sheet at the end of the month:

Income Statement for ABC Widgets for Month Ending 1/31/2XXX

Income	
Widget sales	$4,700
Total Sales	**$4,700**
Cost of Goods Sold	
Widget material	$705
Widget labor	$940
Total Cost of Goods Sold	**$1,645**
Gross Profit	**$3,055**
Fixed Expenses	
Advertising	$1,000
Automobile	$100
Bank charges	$10
Insurance	$100
Office supplies	$25
Owner's compensation	$750
Rent	$500
Total Fixed Expenses	**$2,485**
Net Profit	**$570**

Balance Sheet for ABC Widgets as of 1/31/2XXX

Assets		Liabilities	
Bank account	$5,570	Accounts payable	$0
Accounts receivable	$0		
Inventory	$0	**Equity**	
Equipment	$0	Owner's equity	$5,000
		Retained earnings	$570
		Total Equity	**$5,570**
Total Assets	**$5,570**	**Liabilities & Earnings**	**$5,570**

© *JIST Works*

XYZ Gadgets

I.M. Good's Brother, Notso, started a business the same month: XYZ Gadgets. Notso also started with a $5,000 investment. Notso's opening balance sheet for XYZ was identical to ABC's balance sheet.

Notso made some different management decisions. He spent very little time and money marketing his new business; as a result, his sales are less than he had hoped for. He had to pay high prices for materials because he didn't take advantage of volume discounts. His labor costs were high because he didn't hire experienced employees; the inexperienced staff was slow in producing gadgets. Notso didn't pay himself a salary. He ended the month with a $10 loss.

During the month, Notso collected $1,500 in cash sales and paid $675 in COGS and $835 in fixed expenses. His ending bank balance was $4,990.

Notso posted a loss of $10 to retained earnings.

I.M. and Notso started their businesses on the same day with the same amount of money. In one month, ABC was earning a profit, but XYZ was suffering a loss. Is XYZ worth less than ABC?

Income Statement for XYZ Gadgets for Month Ending 1/31/2XXX

Income	
Gadget sales	$1,500
Total Sales	**$1,500**
Cost of Goods Sold	
Gadget material	$300
Gadget labor	$375
Total Cost of Goods Sold	**$675**
Gross Profit	**$825**
Fixed Expenses	
Advertising	$100
Automobile	$100
Bank charges	$10
Insurance	$100
Office supplies	$25
Owner's compensation	$0
Rent	$500
Total Fixed Expenses	**$835**
Net Profit	**($10)**

Balance Sheet for XYZ Gadgets as of 1/31/2XXX

Assets		Liabilities	
Bank account	$4,990	Accounts payable	$0
Accounts receivable	$0		
Inventory	$0	**Equity**	
Equipment	$0	Owner's equity	$5,000
		Retained earnings:	($10)
		Total Equity	**$4,990**
Total Assets	**$4,990**	**Liabilities & Equity**	**$4,990**

Cash vs. Credit

In the prior examples, ABC's transactions were all made in cash: Cash sales were deposited into the bank account, and cash expenses were paid from the bank account. Here's what that balance sheet looked like:

Balance Sheet for ABC Widgets as of 1/31/2XXX

Assets		Liabilities	
Bank account	$5,570	Accounts payable	$0
Accounts receivable	$0		
Inventory	$0	**Equity**	
Equipment	$0	Owner's equity	$5,000
		Retained earnings	$570
		Total Equity	**$5,570**
Total Assets	**$5,570**	**Liabilities & Equity**	**$5,570**

Take a look at what would happen if ABC had the *same amount of sales and expenses,* but incurred accounts receivable for some of those sales and accounts payable for some of those expenses.

- Remember, sales totaled $4,700. Assume that $4,000 was paid in cash and $700 remained in A/R.

- Expenses (COGS & fixed) totaled $4,130. Assume that $3,000 was paid in cash and $1,130 remained in A/P.

- The bank account had $5,000 in cash at the beginning of the month. Add $4,000 in cash sales and subtract $3,000 in expenses paid. The ending bank balance is $6,000.

- The accounts receivable balance is $700. The accounts payable balance is $1,130.

- The income statement reflects no changes, and retained earnings are still $570. The new balance sheet would look like this:

Balance Sheet for ABC Widgets as of 1/31/2XXX

Assets		Liabilities	
Bank account	$6,000	Accounts payable	$1,130
Accounts receivable	$700		
Inventory	$0	**Equity**	
Equipment	$0	Owner's equity	$5,000
		Retained earnings	$570
		Total Equity	**$5,570**
Total Assets	**$6,700**	**Liabilities & Equity**	**$6,700**

© JIST Works

The business has increased assets and increased liabilities, but the *equity* of the business did not change.

The Chart of Accounts

In a business, transactions occur daily. For ease in identifying all of the accounts a business may use, a listing or *chart of accounts* is created. These accounts often are numbered for easy identification. If you created a personal chart of accounts, it might look like this:

Assets
100 Bank Account
110 House
120 Car

Liabilities
200 Home Mortgage
210 Auto Loan

Equity
300 Home Equity
310 Auto Equity
333 Profit (Loss)

Income
400 Salary Income

Expenses
510 Mortgage Payment
520 Food
530 Utilities
540 Insurance
550 Auto Payment
560 Miscellaneous

Companies create their own charts of accounts, relative to the way they do business. Throughout the year, they can add new accounts to their charts as necessary. An accountant or bookkeeper can help a business establish a chart of accounts that meets its needs. A simple chart of accounts follows:

Assets
100 Regular Checking Account
105 Payroll Checking Account
110 Petty Cash on Hand
115 Trade Accounts Receivable
150 Equipment
155 Furniture and Fixtures
160 Small Tools
180 Inventory on Hand

Liabilities
200 Trade Accounts Payable
205 Payroll Taxes Payable
210 Bank Note Payable
250 Note Payable: Owner

Equity
300 Owner's Contribution
399 Retained Earnings: Year to Date

Income
400 Sales Income
401 Misc. Income

Expenses
500 Accounting
502 Automobile Expense
505 Dues and Subscriptions
508 Depreciation
510 Fees: Bank Charges & Misc.
515 Insurance: Business
516 Insurance: Health
520 Interest Expense
525 Labor: Payroll Expense
526 Labor: Employee Benefits
530 Materials
545 Miscellaneous
550 Owner's Compensation
560 Repair & Maint.
570 Taxes
550 Utilities

A Picture in Review

Let's review what we've learned so far. There are five types of accounts:

1. Assets (what you own)

2. Liabilities (what you owe)

3. Equity (net worth)

4. Income

5. Expenses

Balance Sheet

Assets   Liabilities
        + Equity

Assets = Liabilities + Equity

- Contains assets, liabilities, and equity
- Reports net worth as of a specific date
- Must balance

Income

Income
− Expenses

= Net Profit (Loss)

- Contains income and expenses
- Reports operating profit or loss for a specific period of time

If a business earns a profit, equity increases.

If a business suffers a loss, equity decreases.

Profit or loss is posted to the balance sheet in an equity account called retained earnings.

Retained Earnings Accumulate

You know there is a relationship between income statements and balance sheets: Profit or loss from the income statement is posted to the balance sheet as retained earnings. In the first month of operations, profit or loss and retained earnings will be the same. Each month thereafter, the profit or loss amount from the monthly income statement is added to the prior retained earnings balance.

© JIST Works

Exercise #2

In this exercise, you will create financial statements. Fill in the blanks; then enter the information onto the worksheet on the following page.

1. The name of your imaginary person is _____. Enter this name at the top of both the balance sheet and the income statement.

2. Your person brings home a salary of $_____ each month. Enter this amount on the income statement. If your person has other income, identify this also.

3. Your person is buying a _____. The purchase price is $_____ (asset), and it is being purchased with a down payment of $_____ (equity) and a loan for the balance of $_____ (liability). Enter these amounts on the balance sheet.

4. The monthly household expenses for your person are the following:

Housing expense	$ _____
Food	_____
Utilities	_____
Insurance	_____
Car payment	_____
Daycare	_____
_____	_____
_____	_____
_____	_____
_____	_____
_____	_____
_____	_____

   Enter these amounts where they belong on the income statement.

5. If you'd like, your person is also purchasing a _____. The purchase price is $_____, and it is being purchased with a down payment of $_____ and a loan for the balance of $_____. Enter these amounts on the balance sheet. If your person owns anything else or owes anything else, include these amounts, too.

6. Total your income statement and determine if your person ends with a profit or loss. Remember to reflect this amount on the balance sheet.

7. Now total your balance sheet. Remember that *the balance sheet must balance*. If it doesn't, try to determine what is missing.

   HINT: Did your person end with a profit or loss in number 6? Where did that cash go—into a checking account? Did you remember to include a checking account on the balance sheet?

Exercise #2 Worksheet

_____

Balance Sheet as of 1/31/2XXX

Assets   Liabilities

_____ $ _____   _____ $ _____

_____ $ _____   _____ $ _____

_____ $ _____   _____ $ _____

_____ $ _____   _____ $ _____

                          Equity (net worth)

                          _____ $ _____

                          _____ $ _____

                          _____ $ _____

Total Assets $ _____   Liabilities & Equity $ _____

_____

Income Statement for Period Ending 1/31/2XXX

Income

_____ $ _____

_____ $ _____

_____ $ _____

Expenses

_____ $ _____

_____ $ _____

_____ $ _____

_____ $ _____

_____ $ _____

_____ $ _____

_____ $ _____

_____ $ _____

Profit (Loss) $ _____

© JIST Works

Summing Up

The following are typical questions lenders and accountants ask when analyzing financial statements. Keep them in mind when you review your own:

1. Do assets exceed liabilities? Is there a positive or negative net worth?

2. Does it appear that the values assigned to the assets are reasonable? Assets are posted at their purchase price and adjusted to market price as necessary. Have reasonable adjustments been made? Do adjustments need to be made?

3. Are the assets things that can be sold quickly if necessary? What type of assets are they? How well do they hold their value?

4. Do assets exceed liabilities by a large margin? If some assets had to be sold (liquidated) to pay debts, what would remain?

5. Comparing income to expenses and liabilities, does it seem that money is being spent well?

6. If the company suffered a sudden reduction or fluctuation in income, are there monthly expenses that could be reduced or eliminated easily?

7. Are there large swings in expenses that do not correspond to swings in sales? Does it appear that the company is not controlling operating expenses?

8. Do accounts receivable greatly exceed an average month of sales? If so, chances are good that receivables are not being collected in a timely manner. The older receivables become, the more difficult they are to collect.

9. Do accounts payable greatly exceed an average month of operating expenses? If so, chances are good that bills are not being paid on time. This could result in suppliers no longer extending credit or delivering goods, utilities being disconnected, and loans being called.

10. Are there unexplained accounts payable, such as loans or notes?

11. How much money does the owner have invested in the business? How does this compare to overall debt? Is the company being operated using nothing but OPM (other people's money)?

12. How much salary is the owner taking out of the business? How does this compare to the profit or loss of the business?

Financial statements are excellent management tools. Learn to understand them and use them.

From Dream to Reality

Turning your self-employment dream into reality can be both exhilarating and a bit frightening. This book was written to take some of the mystery out of the process of starting your own business. In this book, we've looked at some of the reasons people decide to become self-employed and why some businesses fail. We've helped you define your dream and understand how to finance it. We've shown you how to set goals and create action plans to achieve them. We've given you the worksheets to price your products and services and the steps to market your business. We've provided information about legal forms of business, insurance, cash-flow management, record-keeping, and financial statements.

Each chapter for this book gives you information about a different aspect of your small business. Consider each aspect and how it applies to your business idea. As you plan your business, write down your ideas step by step. Use this document as the basis for your business plan—your personal guide to starting your own business. (See the Appendix for an example of the form your business plan should take.) Your business plan will help keep you grounded as your dream becomes a reality. Use it to communicate your ideas to other people. As your business grows, you should review and update your business plan to accommodate changes.

Self-employment has many rewards; among them is the satisfaction of having a dream and turning it into something real. Good luck on your journey from dream to reality.

© JIST Works

Appendix

Business Plan

Cathy's Cleaning Service, Inc.

Cathy Smith, President
P.O. Box 0000
Anytown, IN 40000
(317) 000-0000
Cathy@ccsi-anytown.com
www.ccsi-anytown.com

Table of Contents

Page

Cathy's Cleaning Service, Inc.
Business Plan

Introduction

Description of Business

Cathy's Cleaning Service, Inc. (CCSI) is a full-service residential and commercial cleaning company. The business has been owned and operated by Cathy Smith since June 2XXX and is a Sub-S corporation, incorporated in June, 2XXX. The business is operated out of Cathy Smith's home office. The mailing address is P.O. Box 0000, Anytown, IN, 40000. The business phone number is (317) 000-0000.

In June 2XXX, Cathy Smith was a mother of two school-age children and a full-time homemaker when she began cleaning homes for neighbors. Within six months, Cathy was regularly cleaning two residences and had one commercial property contract. She hired her mother and two sisters as part-time employees and has since added to her staff.

Currently, CCSI has three full-time and four part-time employees who work in teams to provide services to clients. Two of the full-time employees and three of the part-time employees make up the commercial cleaning department, and the remaining employees operate in the residential cleaning department.

Commercial contracts are awarded annually, and residential cleaning is done on an ongoing basis unless a homeowner wishes to make a change.

The business goal of CCSI is to provide high-quality residential and commercial cleaning services to customers at a reasonable price which will allow the corporation and its owners to recognize a profit. It is also the mission of the company to foster a healthy working environment, to pay competitive and fair wages to its employees, and to encourage employees to develop a healthy balance between work and family commitments.

The company owner recently completed a business planning course to improve her ability to analyze and monitor pricing and produce long- and short-term cash-flow projections. Additionally, it is the intention to send the owner and one manager to a personnel management course. A short-term capital equipment loan is required to add industrial vacuums and other cleaning equipment, thereby allowing the firm to grow by taking on more commercial contracts.

© *JIST Works*

Marketing

Service Description

CCSI offers residential and light commercial cleaning. For residential customers, each job is bid according to the size of the home, the number of individuals residing in the home, and the scope of services required. The homeowner can choose from three service packages. These are outlined below:

- Residential Cleaning #1—Frequency of visits: 1-4 times per month. Includes dusting of all surfaces, vacuuming all carpeted areas, sweeping and mopping all vinyl or tile floor areas, complete bathroom cleaning, loading dirty dishes into a dishwasher (no hand washing dishes), up to three full loads of laundry (washed, dried, folded, and stacked), general light housecleaning.

- Residential Cleaning #2—Frequency of visits: 1-4 times per month. Includes dusting of all surfaces, vacuuming all carpeted areas, sweeping and mopping all vinyl or tile floor areas, complete bathroom cleaning, general light housecleaning.

- Residential Cleaning #3—Frequency of visits: One-time cleaning. Includes all of the services offered in package #1, plus window washing (inside only) and oven cleaning. This cost of this package is an actual per-hour cost of $20.00 per hour per cleaning person.

The most commonly purchased residential package is #1. Package #2 is usually ordered by the single customer or the customer who may not work full time outside of the home. Package #3 is most often ordered for special occasions, such as weddings or family reunions.

Custom packages are available for customers who have special needs.

Commercial cleaning is bid on a custom basis. The owners or property managers of a commercial building will meet with the owner of CCSI and decide on the frequency of visits and services to be offered. Commonly, the services performed in commercial buildings include emptying trash and ash receptacles, vacuuming carpeted areas, damp mopping vinyl and tile floor areas, and cleaning rest rooms. The professional cleaners of CCSI will not remove or disturb anything atop desks or other personal work areas. Work surfaces, computers, and other electronic equipment will be lightly dusted but not disturbed. All bids for services will be prepared by Cathy Smith.

Market Description

CCSI is located on the near East side of Anytown. The target markets for cleaning services are the residential and commercial customers located on the East and near East sides of Anytown.

The primary residential target customers are families who have both parents working outside the home and who have two or more children. According to *American Demographic* magazine, 43 percent of families of four or larger in which both parents are employed outside the home utilize a professional housecleaning service at least once a month. Of that 43 percent, 51 percent prefer to use a local, privately owned service as opposed to a franchise operation. They state that the reasons for this preference are more dependable service, greater ability to customize services, and more flexible working agreements.

The second target market for residential customers is the single executive. *American Demographic* magazine finds that 37 percent of singles earning an annual income of $40,000 or greater utilize a cleaning service at least one time per month.

According to the 2XXX census report for Anytown, 22 percent of all metropolitan Anytown families of four or larger in which both parents are working outside the home live in the near East side and the East side neighborhoods of Anytown. Only 7 percent of the single executives earning annual incomes of $40,000 or greater reside in this same geographic area.

The commercial market CCSI targets is small office buildings that employ 50 or fewer employees. Larger offices tend to utilize large, franchise cleaning services, and very large, multi-business office buildings often have on-staff cleaning services. Industrial buildings are often quite difficult and time-consuming to clean and are not included in the target market for CCSI.

According to the *Commercial Real Estate Update* (local) magazine, the near East side of Anytown contains more than 30 percent of all small commercial office buildings in the downtown or near downtown areas.

Competition

As of December 31, 2XXX, only two privately-owned cleaning services and no franchise services specifically serviced this geographic area of Anytown. Comparatively, 27 privately-owned services and four large franchise services target the North, Northwest, and Northeast areas of metropolitan Anytown. The South, Southeast, and Southwest areas are serviced by another 15 companies, and the West side of town is targeted by another 12 companies. Even though the East and near East side neighborhoods do not make up the largest portion of the target residential customer, the lack of existing competition and the existing contacts CCSI has established make this a very good market in which to sell its services. The facts that CCSI has an office located on the near East side and that all of its employees live on the East side allow CCSI to be more responsive to customer needs.

Most commercial cleaning services prefer to bid on the larger multi-office office buildings, and a survey conducted by CCSI and mailed to local office buildings found that the smaller buildings have had difficulty finding services willing to clean their offices.

CCSI offers service to an area that is poorly serviced at this time. CCSI also offers custom cleaning services tailored to the specific size of each location and the services requested by the individual customer—something the larger franchise firms do not offer. For residential and commercial customers alike, the fact that CCSI has established a reputation for honest, dependable cleaning people is quite attractive. All employees are bonded, and a police background check is performed prior to hire to ensure high-quality employees. Supervisors are assigned to monitor work crews, thereby providing added security for the customer.

Marketing Strategy

CCSI markets its cleaning services through advertisements in the local *Near Eastside Neighbor* and *Anytown East* newspapers. Additionally, five local church bulletins are used to advertise services. Fliers are posted at four local beauty shops, one local grocery store, and two service stations. A referral program is being offered to existing customers whereby an existing customer who refers a new customer gets a $25 discount on future cleaning services.

Through a local property management company, which manages seventy single-family rental units, one free housecleaning will be awarded (program to begin next month) to a resident who wins this service in a semiannual drawing (all residents who pay their rent early or on time for six months in a row are eligible for the drawing). In the commercial buildings CCSI cleans, one free residential cleaning will be awarded per year to each customer to be given away as the commercial building owner/manager wishes (such as to employees as an "employee of the year" award). Also, cleaning gift certificates for $25, $50, $75, and $100 will be offered to commercial accounts as gifts for employees or preferred customers. Of course, these gift certificates will also be available to residential customers. Once every quarter, all residential and commercial customers will receive a newsletter outlining all current marketing programs.

Word-of-mouth advertising still remains the most effective method of growth for CCSI. All customer suggestions are responded to in writing, and all phone calls are returned within 24 hours. By paying special attention to all customers and frequently (at least once a quarter) contacting all customers by telephone or in person to see if they remain satisfied with the level of services offered, CCSI continues to build a loyal clientele.

Organization

Quality Control

CCSI recognizes the importance of delivering high-quality service in order to maintain a loyal customer base. In order to ensure that cleaning is done to the high standards of CCSI, supervisors regularly inspect the work performed. For residential customers who contract CCSI to clean regularly, at least one cleaning per month is supervised by a manager. For residential customers who contract a single or special-event cleaning, every work crew is headed by a manager who supervises the cleaning. Every commercial work crew is accompanied by a manager who supervises the cleaning of office buildings.

Work crews are scheduled weekly. Two full-time and three part-time employees are regularly scheduled to perform on the commercial contracts. One full-time and one part-time employee regularly clean residential properties. Cathy Smith regularly accompanies work crews as a supervisor. Each work crew has a checklist that must be reviewed before leaving the work site. The checklist ensures that all services contracted are actually performed. The crew leader signs the checklist and becomes responsible for any discrepancies reported by the customer. All cleaning products are provided by CCSI unless a customer specifically requests that a certain product be used. This ensures consistent use of high-quality cleaning products.

CCSI's quarterly contact with every customer allows customers to voice any concerns or complaints they may have regarding the quality of work performed. Customer suggestions are always considered and implemented whenever possible.

Legal Structure

CCSI is a Sub-S corporation, incorporated in June, 2XXX. The business is operated by the sole owner, Cathy Smith. CCSI originally started doing business in 2XXX as a sole proprietorship and converted to a Sub-S for limited liability protection.

Insurance

CCSI carries business liability insurance through Mr. Allen Green of the ABC Insurance Agency. The insurance underwriter is AmerInsurance.

Additionally, all employees of CCSI are bonded. Workers' Compensation and a life insurance policy on Cathy Smith are also sold to CCSI by the same agency.

Management

Cathy Smith is the President and General Manager of CCSI. Her background includes supervisory positions for over 10 years, managing as many as 15 employees in a manufacturing environment. Cathy left the job market for 10 years when she married and had two children, and she began CCSI when her youngest child started first grade.

Cathy hires and trains employees, schedules residential and commercial cleaning, purchases supplies, negotiates contracts, markets the company, and manages all accounts receivable and payable. Each cleaning crew has a crew leader who immediately supervises all work, and each division has a manager who takes responsibility for supervising the crew leaders. Additionally, Cathy acts as a manager in both divisions.

The manager in the commercial cleaning division, Sarah Jones, has five years of experience working as a manager for a national franchise cleaning service. Sarah has worked for CCSI since October, 2XXX.

The residential cleaning division manager, Mary Murphy, has two years of experience as the head of housekeeping services for a large local hotel. Mary has been employed with CCSI since January, 2XXX.

Cathy maintains accounts receivable and payable for CCSI. She collects all business-related receipts and maintains the company checkbook and other records. On a quarterly schedule, Cathy turns these records over to a bookkeeper, who prepares quarterly profit and loss statements. Once a year, a Certified Public Accountant prepares the company taxes and generates a full set of financial statements.

Actual payroll generation and payroll tax records are maintained by PAYCHECKS, Inc., a payroll service. Payroll is generated on the fifteenth and last day of each month.

Advisors

Martha White, CPA, prepares taxes and annual financial statements for CCSI. Ms. White is in private practice with an office located at 123 Main Street, Anytown. John Kennedy, a local attorney with Mayor, Jones, and Smith, is CCSI's attorney. Mr. Kennedy advised CCSI to convert to a Sub-S corporation and filed all the appropriate paperwork with the Secretary of State. Annually, Cathy meets with both Ms. White and Mr. Kennedy to review the status of the company and to discuss any updates or changes that need to be made.

Cathy has also compiled a group of four volunteers who serve as an advisory committee. Once a year, Cathy meets with these advisors to discuss her business strategies and update her business plan. Three of the four advisors are retired executives who offer their expertise based on many years of small business experience. The fourth advisor is a local businesswoman who manages a financial services business. Two of her four advisors are also CCSI customers.

Financial Information

Use of Funds

Use of loan proceeds will be as follows:

Loan Request: $1,000.00

Use of funds is for permanent working capital. A cash-flow projection, which demonstrates that this influx of cash will allow CCSI to service more residential and commercial customers, follows. The projection outlines that the increase in sales will allow CCSI to purchase additional capital equipment beginning in the fourth month. The cash-flow projections also demonstrate an adequate ability to service the debt incurred by this loan.

The proposed loan will be secured with a first security interest in the assets of the business, as well as a personal guaranty from Cathy Smith. CCSI has no business debt at this time and owns equipment with a net value (net of accumulated depreciation) of $3,500.00.

Cash-Flow Assumptions

The first assumption of the cash-flow projection is that all existing business will be retained in the next 12 months. New residential business will be in the form of one house in month 2, an additional house in month 4, a third new house in month 6, and a minor increase in rates in month 10 for a total new residential business income of $1,680.

New commercial business consists of one new building in month 3, a second new building in month 5, and a slight increase in all commercial rates reflected in months 9-12. Total new commercial income for the year is $4,000.

The operating expenses related to new business income are reflected as 68 percent of new residential income and 69 percent of new commercial income.

This assumption is based on historical operating percentages. All fixed expenses remain the same. Loan payments begin in month 3 and are calculated at 10 percent interest for a 12-month term.

Cathy's Cleaning Service _____ Business Plan Pg. 7

© *JIST Works*

Capital equipment purchases will be begin in month 4 with the purchase of three new vacuum cleaners and will include the addition of a floor waxing unit in month 8.

Cathy's Cleaning Service, Inc.

12-Month Cash-Flow Forecast	1	2	3	4	5	6
Beginning Cash Balance	$0	$1,110	$1,239	$1,342	$1,114	$948
Cash Inflow						
Existing Business	$2,470	$2,470	$2,470	$2,470	$2,470	$2,470
Loan Proceeds	$1,000					
Owner Contributions						
New Residential Business		$60	$60	$120	$120	$180
New Commercial Business			$200	$200	$400	$400
Total Cash Inflow	$3,470	$2,530	$2,730	$2,790	$2,990	$3,050
Cash Outflow						
Existing Operating Expenses	$1,643	$1,643	$1,643	$1,643	$1,643	$1,643
New Residential Operating Exp	$0	$41	$41	$82	$82	$122
New Commercial Operating Exp	$0	$0	$138	$138	$276	$276
Office Space	$68	$68	$68	$68	$68	$68
Utilities	$15	$15	$15	$15	$15	$15
Office Supplies	$10	$10	$10	$10	$10	$10
Business Insurance	$25	$25	$25	$25	$25	$25
Auto Expense	$50	$50	$50	$50	$50	$50
Auto Insurance	$35	$35	$35	$35	$35	$35
Pager	$14	$14	$14	$14	$14	$14
Loan Payments			$88	$88	$88	$88
Owner's Compensation	$500	$500	$500	$500	$500	$500
Capital Purchase-Vacuum Clnrs				$350	$350	$350
Capital Purchase-Floor Waxer						
Total Cash Outflow	$2,360	$2,401	$2,627	$3,018	$3,156	$3,196
Monthly change in cash	$1,110	$129	$103	($228)	($166)	($146)
Ending Cash Balance	$1,110	$1,239	$1,342	$1,114	$948	$802

Cathy's Cleaning Service _____ Business Plan Pg. 8a

Cathy's Cleaning Service, Inc.

12-Month Cash-Flow Forecast	7	8	9	10	11	12	Totals
Beginning Cash Balance	$802	$1,006	$710	$945	$1,186	$1,427	
Cash Inflow							
Existing Business	$2,470	$2,470	$2,470	$2,470	$2,470	$2,470	$29,640
Loan Proceeds							$1,000
Owner Contributions							
New Residential Business	$180	$180	$180	$200	$200	$200	$1,680
New Commercial Business	$400	$400	$500	$500	$500	$500	$4,000
Total Cash Inflow	$3,050	$3,050	$3,150	$3,170	$3,170	$3,170	$36,320
Cash Outflow							
Existing Operating Expenses	$1,643	$1,643	$1,643	$1,643	$1,643	$1,643	$19,716
New Residential Operating Exp	$122	$122	$122	$136	$136	$136	$1,142
New Commercial Operating Exp	$276	$276	$345	$345	$345	$345	$2,760
Office Space	$68	$68	$68	$68	$68	$68	$816
Utilities	$15	$15	$15	$15	$15	$15	$180
Office Supplies	$10	$10	$10	$10	$10	$10	$120
Business Insurance	$25	$25	$25	$25	$25	$25	$300
Auto Expense	$50	$50	$50	$50	$50	$50	$600
Auto Insurance	$35	$35	$35	$35	$35	$35	$420
Pager	$14	$14	$14	$14	$14	$14	$168
Loan Payments	$88	$88	$88	$88	$88	$88	$880
Owner's Compensation	$500	$500	$500	$500	$500	$500	$6,000
Capital Purchase–Vacuum Clnrs							$1,050
Capital Purchase–Floor Waxer		$500					$500
Total Cash Outflow	$2,846	$3,346	$2,915	$2,929	$2,929	$2,929	$34,652
Monthly change in cash	$204	($296)	$235	$241	$241	$241	$1,668
Ending Cash Balance	$1,006	$710	$945	$1,186	$1,427	$1,668	$1,668

Cathy's Cleaning Service _____ Business Plan Pg. 8b

© JIST Works

Recommended Resource List

Books

Brabec, B. *Homemade Money-How to Select, Start, Manage, Market and Multiply the Profits of a Business At Home.* Cincinnati: Betterway, 1997.

Cook, M. *Home Business Big Business: The Definitive Guide to Starting and Operating On-Line and Traditional Home-Based Ventures.* New York: Macmillan, 1998.

Covey, Steven. *Principle-Centered Leadership.* New York: Simon & Schuster, 1992.

Covey, Steven. *The Seven Habits of Highly Effective People.* New York: Simon & Schuster, 1990.

Edwards, P., & S. Edwards and L. Clampitt-Douglas. *Getting Business To Come To You: A Complete Do-It-Yourself Guide to Attracting All the Business You Can Enjoy.* New York: Penguin Putnam, Inc., 1998.

Edwards, P., & S. Edwards and L. Rohrbough, *Making Money in Cyberspace,* New York: J.P. Tarcher/Putnam, 1998

Kem, C., and T. Hoffman Wolfgram. *Run Your Own Home Business (Here's How).* New York: McGraw-Hill, 1998.

Levinson, J. *Guerrilla Marketing: Secrets For Making Profits from Your Small Business.* New York: Houghton Mifflin, 1998.

McAleese, T. *Money: How to Get It, Keep It, and Make It Grow.* Broomall: Chelsea House, 1997.

McKain, S. *All Business Is Show Business: Strategies for Earning Standing Ovations From Your Customers,* Nashville: Rutledge Hill Press, 2002.

Ries, A., & J. Trout. *Marketing Warfare.* New York: McGraw-Hill, 1997.

Stansell, K. *Bootstrapper's Success Secrets: 151 Tactics for Bulding Your Business on a Shoestring Budget.* Franklin Lakes: Career Press, 1997.

Stolze, W. *Start Up: An Entrepreneur's Guide to Launching and Managing a New Business.* Franklin Lakes: Career Press, 1999.

Web Sites

http://www.entrepreneur.com—Includes feature articles and columns from *Entrepreneur Magazine.*

http://www.entreworld.org—An online resource for small business owners, the EntreWorld search engine delivers useful information, guidance, and contacts for the entrepreneur.

http://www.inc.com—This magazine and corresponding Web site on entrepreneurship provide hands-on advice, case studies, and overviews on the state of small business in the U.S.

http://www.irs.gov—The Internal Revenue Service Web site offers helpful tax information for small businesses as well as individuals.

http://www.quicken.com—Resources at the Quicken site for the small business sector cover areas such as taxes and accounting, starting a business, office technology, and legal issues.

http://www.sba.gov—Find resources and a FAQ from the Small Business Administration on starting up a small business.

http://www.smallbizhelp.net—A help center for small or home-based business owners, anyone who wants to start a small or home-based business, entrepreneurs, independent publishers, and mail-order dealers. This site offers marketing newsletters, below-wholesale product sources, success books, Internet marketing resources, home-based business opportunities, and more.

http://www.businesstown.com—This small-business site contains hundreds of key links, plus information on topics like firing employees, selling your business, marketing, and doing taxes.

© *JIST Works*

Index

D

E

© JIST Works

© JIST Works

See us on the World Wide Web: www.jist.com

Here Are Just Some of Our Products!

JIST publishes hundreds of books, videos, software products, and other items. Some of our best-selling career and educational products are presented here. You can order these books through any bookstore or Internet bookseller's site or by calling 1-800-648-JIST.

Check out JIST's Web site at www.jist.com for tables of contents and free chapters from these and other products.

Effective Communication Skills, Second Edition
Essential Skills for Success in Work and Life
Marsha Ludden

This workbook covers the basics of getting your message across in casual conversation or public speaking, in e-mail or letters, and at work or with friends. Exercises, reviews, and samples help to reinforce skills and concepts.

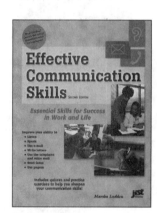

ISBN 1-56370-852-3 / Order Code LP-J8523 / **$8.95**

Telecommuting Success
A Practical Guide for Staying in the Loop While Working Away from the Office
Michael Dziak

Become a power telecommuter! This book's worksheets, insights from industry pros, and Web resources can help you to successfully work from a home office. It shows you how to avoid telecommuting's negatives and gives you information on accomplishing more, communicating more effectively, and staying visible to your coworkers.

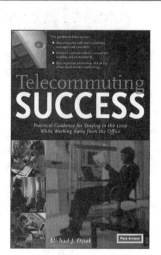

ISBN 1-57112-109-9 / Order Code LP-P1099 / **$16.95**

Call 1-800-648-JIST or Fax 1-800-JIST-FAX

APR 13 2006

See us on the World Wide Web: www.jist.com

Ready, Set, Organize!, Second Edition
A Workbook for the Organizationally Challenged
Pipi Campbell Peterson with Mary Campbell

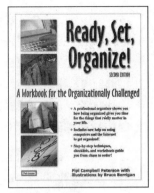

Getting organized doesn't have to be painful! This book is for you if your closet is messy, all of your drawers are "junk drawers," or you can never find your keys. Charts and checklists, as well as realistic examples, make learning to be neat painless and fun. Find out how to use calendars, organize your clothing and personal items, file papers, set up a home office, and more.

ISBN 1-57112-111-0 / Order Code LP-P1110 / **$12.95**

Dare to Change Your Job and Your Life, Second Edition

Carole Kanchier, Ph.D.

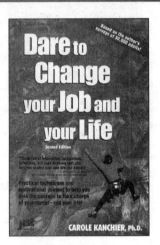

This practical and thought-provoking book challenges you to confront your job and your life. It helps you understand how you and your career grow and change through life and enables you to develop an action plan to take control of your career and your life.

ISBN 1-56370-556-7 / Order Code LP-J5567 / **$16.95**

Getting the Job You Really Want, Fourth Edition

Michael Farr

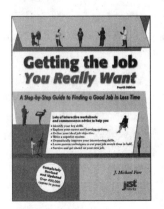

The most widely used workbook on self-directed career planning and job search at schools, colleges, and employment programs in North America!

Offers new information on using the Internet and other technology effectively in the job search. Lots of interactive worksheets and common-sense advice guide readers step-by-step through the process of getting the job they really want.

The techniques presented have helped millions of people find better jobs in less time.

ISBN 1-56370-803-5 / Order Code LP-J8035 / **$12.95**

Call 1-800-648-JIST or Fax 1-800-JIST-FAX